The World's Greatest Motor Competitions

Le Mans

B. T. Batsford Ltd, London

FIRST PUBLISHED 1987

© *Miura Publications Ltd., 1987*

ISBN 0 7134 5453 9

PRODUCED BY MIURA PUBLICATIONS LTD.
TYPESET BY PHOTOSETTING, YEOVIL
PRINTED IN ENGLAND BY WINCANTON LITHO, WINCANTON, SOMERSET
FOR THE PUBLISHERS
B. T. BATSFORD LTD
4 FITZHARDINGE STREET, LONDON, W1H 0AH

Contents

Introduction: Fighting Spirit

Another big 6.0 litre racing engine brought back to life adds to the deafening wall of sound echoing around the pits. Another 200 m.p.h. prototype slamming past rattles the restless shutters of the *Restaurant des Hunaudières*. Another tannoy message trying anxiously to penetrate the endless din from the track goes largely unheard. It is pitch black. It is raining. For drivers and mechanics the race has been 12 hours of hell. There is another complete revolution of the clock to go. There are no thoughts of quitting.

Year in, year out the challenge remains the same. Not so the face of Le Mans. Gone for good are the crude if rugged passenger cars with four seats and a hood. Gone, too, is the patter of feet on tarmac at 4.00 p.m., as surely as the squeal of tortured tyres on poorly surfaced, everyday roads. But the start still *is* at 4.00 p.m. and much of the road still *is* a public one, if surfaced as a race circuit. Since 1923 at least the time and venue have remained constant. Even the now-famous entertainment 'village' was to be found in embryo form the first year, a jazz band and cinema entertaining spectators.

The event has grown bigger in almost all respects, to become the biggest motor race in Europe. But its fascination lies not only in the annual manifestation of that stature. *Les Vingt Quatre Heures du Mans* is more than mere spectacle. It is an unfolding adventure in which men and cars participate. This book explores the mechanical aspect of that adventure through the experience of the Great Marques that have made it possible.

●●●●●

Our story is based on the edge of a cathedral city, the capital of the region of North West France known as La Sarthe after the river which flows through it, a tributary of the Loire. The city was the base for the first-ever Grand Prix, the 'G.P. de l'Automobile Club de France' of 1906. That was held over a circuit to the east of the metropolitan area. Between 1911 and 1913 a 'Grand Prix de France' was held over a circuit to the south, promoted by the Le Mans-based Automobile Club de la Sarthe. This organisation reformed after the war as the Automobile Club de l'Ouest (ACO) and created a 10.73 mile circuit incorporating some of the roads used by the longer, triangular circuit of 1911–13. This was the venue used by the first post-war Grand Prix, held in 1921.

The ACO's new circuit took cars along the 'Route Nationale 158', the main Le Mans – Tours highway from the suburbs of Le Mans at Pontlieue down to the outskirts of Mulsanne village, some five miles of almost dead straight road distant. Having travelled through the woods to within sight of Mulsanne, the cars were taken right, along a minor road in the direction of Arnage as far as the *chemin d'intérêt commun 113*, the road linking Le Mans with the town of Laigne. That road was used to take the cars back to Pontlieue, again offering a long, fast straight.

As well as the 1921 Grand Prix, the post-war Le Mans circuit was used for a *Coupe Internationale des Voiturettes* over the years 1920–22. In 1922 the ACO started planning something rather different. Club Secretary Georges Durand wanted to organise a race that would demonstrate the reliability of touring cars and discussed his ideas with Charles Faroux, Editor of *La Vie Automobile*. Faroux had heard that Emile Coquille, the French agent for the British Rudge-Whitworth automotive parts concern, was interested in promoting a night race to demonstrate the effectiveness of automobile illumination.

Inspiration wasn't far away – a *Bol d'Or* 24-hour race for light cars was held at St. Germain near Paris in 1922. The 24-hour concept was already familiar in the USA, but over the Atlantic had always been promoted in floodlit stadiums. The *Bol d'Or* proved that it was feasible for unlit European road circuits, too.

Faroux drafted the regulations and Coquille put up 100,000FF sponsorship money and a Rudge-Whitworth Cup. Eligible cars had to have four seats (unless under 1100cc) and had to be catalogued touring models of which at least 30 had been constructed, running to original factory specification. The Cup was established as a triennial award, going to the car covering the greatest distance over the first three annual runnings of the event. However, in 1925 a biennial award was instigated and in 1928 the event became, officially, a 24-hour race.

The first six marathons were held over the established 10.73-mile course but in 1929 a short cut was built to eliminate the Pontlieue hairpin, a notorious accident black spot. This shortened the track to 10.15 miles. A more significant alteration came in 1932 when a new road was built to link the start/finish area on the route 113 across to the RN 158 at a point near Terte Rouge. Incorporating an Esses, this link reduced the mileage to 8.38, a distance that would remain consistent through subsequent years until, in 1955, a slight remodelling of a section near Arnage reduced the length to 8.36 miles.

In 1968 a new chicane immediately before the pits increased the circuit's length by a mere five-hundredths of a mile but in 1974 a revised route from Arnage to that 'Virage Ford' chicane, incorporating a number of new bends, increased the length to 8.47 miles. In 1986 Mulsanne Corner was slightly remodelled to accommodate municipal road developments.

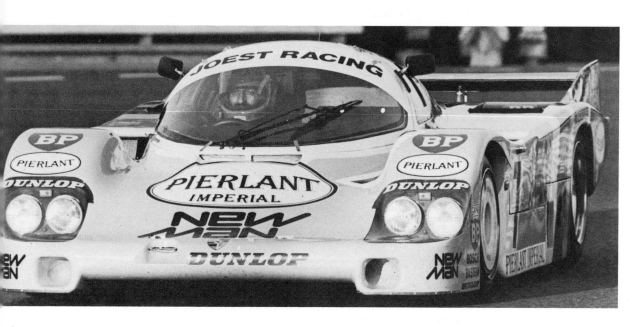

The characteristics of the cars changed far more than the circuit. Those early four-seater tourers were not greatly removed from contemporary racing cars. Inevitably, technological progress put paid to that. It was the Italian, then German state-funded Grand Prix racing programmes of the Thirties that really pushed racing car technology into the realms of science and specialization. That in turn had an impact upon the development of the Le Mans car, once the concept of standard touring cars had been lost.

Just what constitutes a touring car? Any definition is open to a number of different interpretations and naturally glory-seeking motor manufacturers have always been keen to exploit racing techniques. Alfa Romeo's super-successful Le Mans car of the early Thirties was a close relative of the marque's trend-setting contemporary Grand Prix car. In 1937 rear seats and doors became optional and French manufacturers Talbot and Delahaye/Delage developed two-seater versions of their Grand Prix cars for the glory of France. These formed the backbone of the large capacity entry when the race was revived in 1949. By officially allowing the participation of 'prototypes' that year, the ACO was merely accommodating something which already existed: the specialized sports-racing car.

The prototype was at first accepted as an 'exceptional measure' but, quickly established as a feature of Fifties international sports car racing, Le Mans could not turn its back on it without loss of prestige and spectacle. Keeping in line with international sports car racing ensured the 24-hour race featured the fastest, most glamorous sports-racing cars.

This book traces the development of those Le Mans cars from their origins in the tourers of the Twenties. The story concentrates upon the competitors for high overall positions but a full list of class winners is provided in the results section. Each year, the fortunes of every marque represented in the fight for high placings is explored.

The student of Le Mans history seeking further detail is fortunate in having a wealth of contemporary reports to consult. Among the most valuable sources in the English language (and referred to in the research for this book) are *Motor* (previously *The Motor*), *Motor Sport*, *Motoring News* and *Autosport*. Useful earlier books on the race include Georges Fraichard's *The Le Mans Story* published by The Bodley Head in the mid-Fifties and David Hodges' *The Le Mans 24 Hour Race* published by Temple Press in the mid-Sixties.

Le Mans is a ceaseless quest for speed with stamina that has helped build the reputations of some of the foremost manufacturers of sporting cars. This particular account of its history is dedicated to each and every marque which has participated in that quest. In itself, participation is evidence of courage and a fighting spirit.

1923

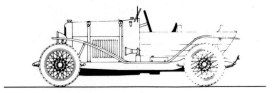

CHENARD & WALCKER, 3-litre
1372.94 miles at 57.20mph

1928

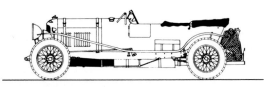

BENTLEY, 4½-litre
1658.60 miles at 69.11mph

EVOLUTION OF THE WINNERS

1932

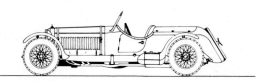

ALFA ROMEO 8C, 2.3-litre s/c
1835.55 miles at 76.48mph

1937

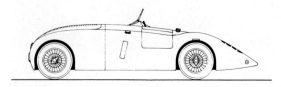

BUGATTI 57G 'TANK', 3.3-litre s/c
2043.03 miles at 85.12mph

1950

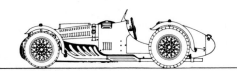

TALBOT-LAGO, 4.5-litre
2153.12 miles at 89.71mph

1955

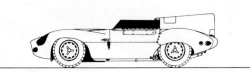

JAGUAR D-TYPE, 3.4-litre
2569.60 miles at 107.07mph

1966

FORD GT40 MK11, 7-litre
3009.35 miles at 125.39mph

1970

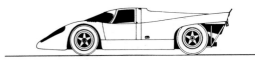

PORSCHE 917K3, 4.5-litre
2863.15 miles at 119.30mph

1959

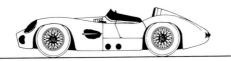

ASTON MARTIN DBR1, 3-litre
2701.65 miles at 112.57mph

1976

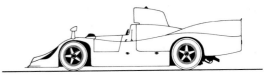

PORSCHE 936, 2.1-litre t/c
2963.89 miles at 123.49mph

1963

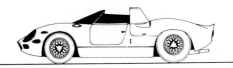

FERRARI 250P, 3-litre
2834.51 miles at 118.10mph

1982

PORSCHE 956, 2.6-litre t/c
3044.15 miles at 126.84mph

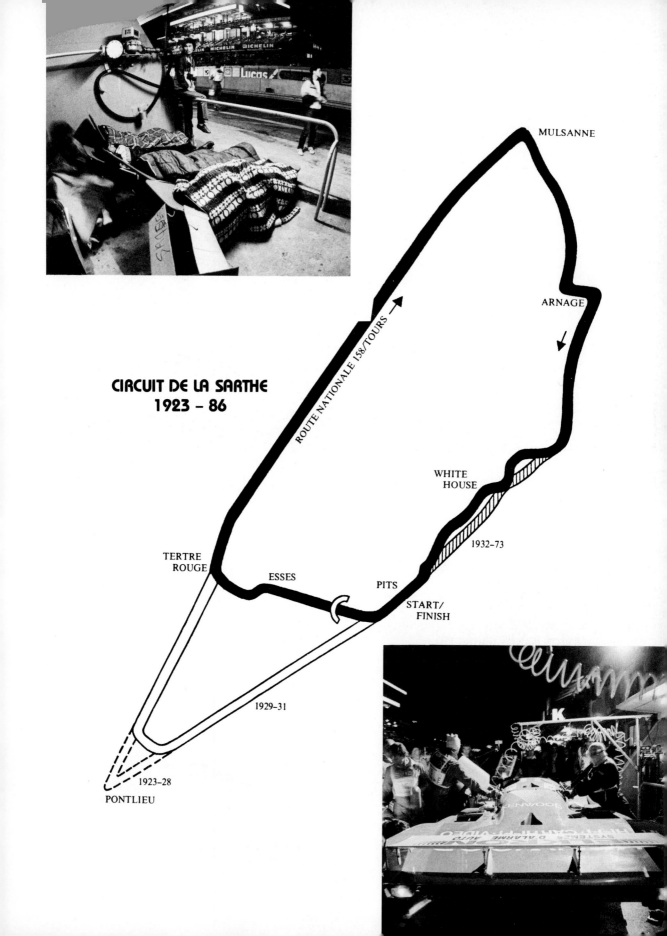

**CIRCUIT DE LA SARTHE
1923 – 86**

MULSANNE

ARNAGE

ROUTE NATIONALE 158/TOURS →

WHITE
HOUSE

1932–73

TERTRE
ROUGE

ESSES

PITS

START/
FINISH

1929–31

1923–28

PONTLIEU

Le Mans is not just another race. It is a special occasion and the preliminaries bring out the showman in each entrant – and, of course, those famous French showgirls!

The build up to the Great Race is faithfully recorded through countless camera lenses. Here US network ABC prepares its own, American interpretation of the scene.

No longer do drivers run across the road to waiting cars – Modern Group C machines have always been started from a conventional dummy grid. One lap behind a pace car, then it's off to a flying start.

The only way to keep track of the leaders throughout a complete lap is on the TV screen. Highlights of the race are broadcast throughout the world, with commentary added from this vantage point overlooking the startline area.

Early stages of the race – the stands are full and there's plenty of action with over 50 cars on the track. Progressively the spectators will drift away and cars will drop by the wayside, and night will fall.

Pit crews play a vital role in the outcome of the race. Even a routine stop takes around two minutes thanks to the compulsory refuelling rate, giving mechanics time to clean the screen and cast an eye over the running gear.

The clock struck four and the mice came running down... The victorious works Porsche 956 was unable to take the flag at the end of the 1982 race as the track had been completely invaded. No matter who wins, the end of the marathon is an excuse for much revelry...

... sometimes those revellers get a little carried away, as witness this scene with '82 winners Ickx and Bell on the ACO balcony. No vantage point is missed as fans crowd in on the ceremony!

Part One
1923 - 39

1923-7

Bentley's famous string of four successive wins did not begin until 1927 but it was the participation of the marque in the formative years that made the new French 24-hour manifestation something more than a local affair. That participation was down to a remarkable privateer, the young, adventure-seeking, British-based Canadian John Duff. Duff fought for Britain in World War One and afterwards got involved in the motor trade in London and continued his quest for adventure at Brooklands. Awarded a Bentley franchise in 1922, he took his first example of Walter Owen Bentley's marque to Brooklands and set 38 international records in two 12-hour shifts, night running not being allowed on the banked circuit. Alas, later that year he broke both ankles flying over the top of the banking in a big 21 litre Benz.

Harsh training got the 28-year-old fit again for the 1923 season and the announcement of the ACO's 24-hour marathon was something he could not resist. The first entry received by Durand was that of Duff. 'W.O.' showed little enthusiasm for the new French concept but agreed to let Frank Clement of his experimental department share Duff's car, which was prepared by Duff's business partner Jack Adlington. W.O. was not alone in his scepticism – two 5.3 litre Excelsiors from neighbouring Belgium were the only other non French runners attracted by the ACO in 1923. They were the biggest capacity cars. In addition, Duff's 3.0 litre Bentley faced three Chenard et Walckers and three La Lorraines of equal capacity and a host of small cars.

It was the Chenard team that made the running, Lagache/Leonard and Bachmann/Dauvergne leading from early on to the finish. The Bentley suffered inadequate brakes. However, it set fastest lap at 66.69 m.p.h. – and also ran out of petrol due to a holed tank which left Duff walking in from Arnage. Clement cycled back with some replenishment and the car finished fifth, behind two 2.0 litre Bignans.

Impressed by the twice-around-the-clock challenge, W.O. offered a greater measure of support for Duff's effort the following year when the Bentley, now with four wheel brakes, was the only foreign car. The line-up of home heroes had strengthened – Chenard entered a 4.0 litre car in addition to a 3.0 litre and La Lorraine went one better by fielding three 4.5 litre runners. In addition, there was a new threat from a 3.2 litre Aries and Bignan had two 3.0 litre cars.

Surprisingly, the big La Lorraines were the least fleet of the big French runners. They and the Duff/Clement Bentley were overshadowed in the early stages but by midnight all the faster machines had retired. On Sunday Duff, overcoming delays due to a jammed gearchange and fragile shock absorbers, overtook the fastest La Lorraine and when it retired soon after 1.00 p.m., the British car was left with a very secure looking lead. However, with victory seemingly in sight the British Racing Green machine lost a lot of time during a precautionary wheel change due to a swollen hub. The delay dropped its average for the last five laps below a statutory minimum so that distance was disallowed . . . and the La Lorraine survivor came within 10 miles of winning.

Later steel filings were found in the Bentley hubs: foul play was suspected. Nevertheless, the car's triumph led to a two-car works team the following year, against which Sunbeam pitted a pair of 3.0 litre cars. There was also a challenge from America in the form of a 3.3 litre Chrysler and another from Italy in the guise of two 3.0 litre Diattos. Duff's success had given the meeting international interest.

Alas, it was a disastrous race for W.O.'s squad, both cars running out of fuel. Duff/Clement got going again by cunning means, only to retire when a carburettor broke off, causing an underbonnet fire. The Sunbeam team, which had duelled with Bentley for the lead in the early stages, also suffered mechanical setback, but brought one car home with a fractured chassis in second place. That car was sandwiched by the victorious French marque: La Lorraine. The other big French cars (a 4.9 litre from Sizaire-Berwick, two 3.9s from Chenard and two 3.0s from Aries), like the

Start of the 1927 race with Clement's 4.4 litre Bentley off to a flying start, chased by Benjafield's similar 3.0 litre car. Photo: Autocar/Quadrant.

other foreign visitors, lacked the necessary stamina. However, the performance of Chenard et Walcker's small capacity (1100cc) cars gave it the Triennial and first Biennial Cups.

Increased international interest was evident once again in 1926 when Willys-Knight shipped two cars over from the USA, a 3.9 litre and 2.8 'Overland'. This year Sunbeam was absent but Bentley was back with a three-strong representation – without Duff. He had gone to the USA in search of alternative excitement. And didn't miss much: all three of W.O.'s runners retired...

But, while Bentley at least came close to a second success, the American cars didn't prove a force to be reckoned with. Of seven big capacity French entries, it was again the La Lorraines which demonstrated the stamina required. A pair of fast 3.8 litre Peugeots and a brace of 3.0 Aries fell by the wayside, leaving La Lorraine with a tremendous one-two-three finish.

La Lorraine rested on its laurels and Peugeot stepped back from the fray, leaving only a solitary Aries to face Bentley in 1927. That elusive second win had to be on the cards, particularly as the marque had a 4.4 litre car alongside two 3.0 models. In the hands of Clement/Callingham, the 4.4 litre went into the lead from the 'off' and was comfortably heading its sister cars when the famous White House multiple accident all but wiped out the entire team. The incident left the Aries ahead of the surviving Davis/Benjafield 3.0 which had lost half-an-hour to repairs by its crew (the mechanics not allowed to assist) but had stood a heavy impact extremely well.

Fuel pump trouble for the Aries cut its advantage to a single lap on Sunday afternoon but it remained the fastest runner. The final twist came at 2.30 p.m. – the Aries broke, handing 'Old Number Seven' its historic triumph, one that further bolstered the international prestige of the race, even if it wasn't recognised as an official 'win'...

1928

To strengthen its claim to be Europe's top sports car manufacturer, Bentley ranged a team of three 4.4 litre cars against which the rest of Europe's factories could but muster a single over 2.0 litre entry – the plucky 3.0 litre Aries. But there was a bigger threat from the New World: five large-capacity cars in the shape of four 4.1 litre Model 72 Chryslers plus a 4.7 litre Stutz Black Hawk.

Stutz had shown its prowess at Indianapolis. The marque founded in the late 1890s by Harry Stutz (who quit after World War One) had been beaten by a more powerful 8.0 litre Hispano-Suiza but had put up such an impressive fight that the winning Hispano-Suiza driver Weymann was moved to back its Le Mans entry. Its Black Hawk speedster was based on its regular 'BB' tourer with 8 cylinder in-line, s.o.h.c. engine, hydraulic brakes and rigid, low slung, semi-elliptic sprung chassis. The car's low centre of gravity and high rigidity endowed it with impressive cornering potential and it boasted a 125 b.h.p. engine and efficient Lockheed brakes. Equipped with a fabric body produced by Weymann's renowned company, the Le Mans car in the hands of Indianapolis winner Bloch and Brisson was on the Bentley pace, trading the lap record in the early stages.

The three Bentleys led from the start but the American car was right with them and it wasn't long before one of the British Racing Green machines fell back with a puncture. Overnight another retired due to a vibration-induced chassis frame fracture causing a water leak. In the lead at midnight, the Stutz was overtaken again by the Barnato/Rubin Bentley before dawn. But the threat of a cracked chassis hung over the surviving British cars...

With one-and-a-half hours to go the Stutz lost two of its three gears. Continuing in top after a lengthy stop, it looked to have handed the race to Barnato/Rubin. However, this 4.4 litre's chassis also cracked. Barnato nursed it home only eight miles ahead of the American entry...

So it was a somewhat fortuitous win for Bentley and Barnato. The company benefactor since 1926 (when his fortune saved it from liquidation), this was 'Babe' Barnato's first visit to La Sarthe and he had elected to drive the 1927 prototype 4.4 litre car. Chairman of the Bentley board, Barnato was a first-rate driver but was content to leave the engineering side of the company to Walter Owen.

W.O.'s 4.4 litre engine wasn't simply an offshoot of the familiar 3.0 litre he designed in 1919 in the light of war time involvement with aero engines. Rather, it was a four-cylinder version of a 6.6 litre in-line six he had introduced in 1925. With shaft driven s.o.h.c. and breathing through 16 valves from two SU carburettors, it developed well in excess of 110 b.h.p.. A plate rather than a cone clutch was used in 1928 but other than that the rolling chassis was the regular ladder frame job with beam axle, semi-elliptic springs and friction dampers front and rear, and four-speed gearbox mounted remote from the power source. With a 3250mm wheelbase the bulky British 'lorry' weighed in at well over 1500kgs and could almost top 100 m.p.h. on the Mulsanne.

While a cracked chassis cost the race of Clement/Benjafield, the puncture that afflicted Birkin/Chassagne had a less dire consequence, even though it cost three hours. That delay was down to the lack of an on-board jack. Birkin tried to drive the heavy car home on the rim but the wheel cried enough, and left him a long walk. Nevertheless, the car recovered to finish fifth, Birkin setting a new lap record in the late stages.

Between the lead battle and the recovering Bentley, Chryslers ran home third and fourth, a worthy result for the marque which had been overshadowed by Stutz for speed and had lost its other two runners, one after only ten laps.

... But that was nine more than the Aries managed. The only 3.0 litre car in the race, it ran its bearings before its s.o.h.c. in-line four had warmed up properly. A sad finale for the French marque that had come so close to toppling Bentley in '27 with its hideous-looking, 'streamline tail' lone entry.

In the wake of the muscle cars the 2.0 litre entries from British Lagonda (three four-cylinder 'Speed Models') and Italian Itala (two brand-new, six-cylinder *Tipo* 65S) were overshadowed by the reliability of a 1.5 litre front-wheel drive British Alvis which came home a splendid sixth. The marque had built a front-wheel drive Grand Prix car in '26 and this year had launched its 1.5 litre four-cylinder road car, also with gearbox ahead of the engine and all-independent suspension.

In fact, Le Mans was notable for the appearance of novel front-wheel drive cars this year, two from Alvis and two from the French Tracta concern, of 1100cc. All finished. Of the 2.0 litre (conventional) runners, Lagonda's only finisher was 11th while Itala managed an eighth place. The 1928 race would be remembered for small capacity, front-wheel drive cars in the classes, and for American cars at the front of the field. But Bentley, appropriately enough, had become the first official winner and moves were afoot to keep it abreast of the new challenge...

1.	4.4 Bentley*	5.	4.4 Bentley
	(Barnato/Rubin)		(Birkin/Chassagne)
2.	4.9 Stutz	6.	1.5 Alvis*
	(Brisson/Bloch)		(Harvey/Purdy)
3.	4.1 Chrysler		* Class winners. Also:
	(Stoffel/Rossignol)	7.	1.1 BNC
4.	4.1 Chrysler		(Dore/Truenet)
	(Ghica/Ghica)	8.	2.0 Italia
			(Benoist/Dauvergne)

1929

There were two trains of thought as to how best to give Bentley more speed. Lap record holder Birkin was attracted by the concept of supercharging. He had a forced induction 4.4 litre running early in '29, but the project ran into many teething troubles, particularly with lubrication. W.O.'s answer was a racing version of his 'Big Six', the 6.6 litre engine upon which the 4.4 had been based. The large in-line six had lent bore and stroke, con rods, pistons and four valve heads to its four-cylinder offshoot and, prepared for racing, offered 200 b.h.p. at the usual modest 3500 r.p.m. – still in the region of 30 b.h.p. per litre.

The Big Six chassis' servo assisted brakes were retained for the new 'Speed Six' which was readied for a debut in May's Brooklands 'Double Twelve', a two-part 24-hour race. The car led for four hours, then its dynamo coupling failed. At Le Mans the following month the new Speed Six was backed up by no less than four regular 4.4 litre cars with suitably strengthened chassis. The race was another Anglo-American affair. This year there were no big capacity continental cars and Faroux called the lack of French representation 'dishonourable'. From England the 'Bentley Boys' were joined by a 4.5 litre Invicta, while from the USA came three Stutz, two Chryslers and a single Du Pont of 5.2 litres.

The first lap told the story: the Barnato/Birkin Speed Six went out on its own in the hands of the company Chairman and the 4.4 litre stablemates kept the Stutzes at bay. However, within the first hour the Howe/Rubin 4.4 was in trouble with its electrics – though to be fair, it should be noted that this car had run a 24-hour race at Montlhery the previous week. Following two magneto changes it was retired at 6.30 p.m.

The other Bentleys were well in command and by 8.00 p.m. had lapped the entire field, save for the fastest Stutz, which had British record breaker Eyston in its crew.

Overnight the Bentley walkover continued relentlessly, while the Stutz effort crumbled. The Brisson/Chiron Stutz caught fire when petrol spilled onto its exhaust. Brisson was out and Chiron's subsequent solo effort ended with a leaking fuel tank. The same fate awaited Eyston's car, costing a likely third place finish.

While Stutz managed only one finisher from three cars, Bentley backed up its superior speed with better reliability, taking a one-two-three-four finish in the carefully staged formation led by the Speed Six. The third and fourth placed cars had been delayed by infuriating bothers but still beat the surviving Stutz (Bouriat/Philippe) which, in fifth place, was over 200 miles behind the Speed Six in which Birkin took another lap record. The performance of the new car was good enough to collect the Index of Performance and Barnato/Birkin were the first drivers to win at an average speed in excess of 70 m.p.h., managing 73.63 m.p.h. on a circuit that had been fractionally abbreviated by the Pontlieue by-pass.

Thoroughly beaten this year, the Americans brought home three cars, the Chryslers finishing sixth and seventh, beaten by the surviving Stutz due to transmission bothers.

The faster Du Pont Model G, with 8-cylinder side valve engine, European-style four-speed gearbox and special aluminium body with distinctive pointed tail, lasted less than four hours. A ballast weight broke through the floor and bent the prop shaft.

Behind the surviving monsters the small car honours went to a Lea Francis of 1500cc. Between the over 4000cc and up to 1500cc runners had been but one entry, a 2.0 litre Lagonda entered by a group of dealers. It had lost its coolant through a leaky cylinder head early in the race. In contrast, the Meadows-engined Lea Francis had done what the 4.5 litre Meadows-engined Invicta failed to do, the big capacity in-line six having run its bearings early on Sunday morning.

The little car was unusual for its supercharged engine. A push rod in-line four, it was beefed up with massive crankshaft and roller bearing big ends, and with improved induction and a big Cozette blower its 1496ccs were coaxed to produce 79 b.h.p. – over 50 b.h.p. per litre. The fleet little S-type car was also light, weighing in at well under 1000kgs. Supercharging was clearly a formula for impressive power per litre with stamina (and little weight penalty). Cause for encouragement for the Birkin faction within the Bentley camp...

1.	6.6 Bentley* (Barnato/Birkin)	5.	5.3 Stutz (Bouriat/Philippe)
2.	4.4 Bentley* (Kidston/Dunfee)	6.	4.1 Chrysler (Stoffel/Benoist)
3.	4.4 Bentley (Benjafield/d'Erlanger)		* Class winners. Also:
		8.	1.5 Lea Francis (Peacock/Newsome)
4.	4.4 Bentley (Clement/Chassagne)	9.	1.0 Tracta (Balart/Debeugny)

1930

By 1930 Benley had two powerful weapons in its armoury: the well-developed Speed Six and Birkin's supercharged 4.4 litre. It was well prepared to tackle the most powerful sports car to emerge from the Twenties – the Type SS Mercedes.

The SS was a development of Ferdinand Porsche's Type S of 1927 – the first real sportscar produced by the Mercedes-Benz combine which had been founded in 1926 through the amalgamation of Daimler and Benz. At its heart was an in-line six of massive 7069cc displacement with shaft driven s.o.h.c. Blown by a two-vane Roots supercharger gear driven from the crankshaft at three times engine speed, the Porsche elephant engine churned out in excess of 200 b.h.p. It propelled a traditional Twenties sports chassis with beam axles, semi-elliptics and mechanical drums. The car won the Formula Libre German Grand Prix at the Nurburgring on its debut in 1928 in the hands of Caracciola.

Although Professor Porsche quit in 1928 (and was succeeded by Hans Nibel), the combination of Caracciola and the SS continued to be a formidable one and a short-chassis version, the SSK, came close to winning the 1929 Monaco Grand Prix against far more agile Grand Prix cars. Britain got a taste of the SSK when Caracciola won the 1929 Belfast TT.

Right from the start of the 1930 Le Mans race Caracciola gave the five-strong Bentley squad something to think about, charging into the lead. On the fourth lap Birkin's new blower Bentley demoted the big white car with an ambitious passing attempt at Mulsanne corner, which left it with a buckled rear mudguard. The twisted metal rubbed against the tyre and soon the supercharged green machine was in the pits. Not long afterwards Birkin suffered a thrown tread.

Barnato was left as the main challenger in a Speed Six. While, with backing from the Hon. Dorothy Paget, Birkin had entered two blowers running on benzole (Birkin/Chassagne and Benjafield/Ramponi), the factory was running three Speed Sixes (Barnato/Kidston, Clement/Watney and Davis/Dunfee). Of Barnato's stable mates, Dunfee went into the sandbanks soon after relieving Davis and there the car was stranded.

The blower Bentleys were unlucky in 1930, the last year the marque would win the race. This is Benjafield's example, rear wing torn by a tyre blowout. Photo: Autocar/Quadrant.

Meanwhile, Barnato/Kidston fought a tremendous duel with Caracciola/Werner, the two cars playing cat and mouse into the night. At midnight the Bentley held a three minute lead but an unscheduled tyre stop put paid to that. Nevertheless, there was worse in store for the German car: it refused to restart from a scheduled pit stop. The dynamo had stopped recharging. The car was *hors de combat*. Rather than see it pushed to the dead car park, Clerk of the Course Faroux suggested it be left in front of its pit as a tribute to its great fight.

In the hands of Bentley, the race fell to the dependable Speed Six models. Birkin had solved the blower model's lubrication problem with a modified sump and managed to set another lap record with his creation, but neither of the Amherst Villers' blown 4.4 litres saw the finish. Both broke on Sunday – valve and piston failure.

Overshadowed by the European battle, Stutz had neither speed nor reliability this year. Its new 32-valve d.o.h.c. engine of 5.3 litres' displacement provided a less than adequate 160 b.h.p. and both its 'DV32's were out by midnight. The hard-trying 'Phillippe's' downfall was an 'off' at Arnage, while Rigal had to bale out of the other car when it caught fire along the Mulsanne straight...

Stutz was the only American challenger this year. The depression was well set in and Le Mans had its smallest turn-out since its inception: 17 cars. Two of the most impressive were 2.3 litre Talbots from England, entered by dealers Fox and Nichol. The Roesch-designed in-line six Talbot engine produced over 80 b.h.p. at 4500 r.p.m. It was a new feature – the marque was noted for its sweet 1.7 litre unit. In a short 14/45 Scout chassis the new unit produced a remarkably fast yet smooth and quiet sports car – which proved good enough to fend off the challenge of a blown 1.8 litre Alfa Romeo to collect splendid third and fourth places overall.

All in all, 1930 was a good year for Britain at Le Mans, Lea Francis again taking the 1500cc honours, this year beating a Bugatti – the first time that marque had been represented in its home race, even though it was a major force in Grand Prix racing. And for Talbot, Alfa Romeo had been no mean rival: its 85-b.h.p. in-line six propelled 6C 1750 had twice won the gruelling Mille Miglia road race through Central Italy. Competition orientated, both Bugatti and Alfa Romeo planned to be back, looking for outright wins in the increasingly prestigious French marathon.

1.	6.6 Bentley* (Barnato/Kidston)		5.	1.8 Alfa Romeo* (Howe/Callingham)
2.	6.6 Bentley (Clement/Whitney)		6.	1.5 Lea Francis* (Peacock/Newsome)
3.	2.3 Talbot* (Lewis/Eaton)			* Class winners. Also:
4.	2.3 Talbot (Hindmarsh/Rose-Richards)		8.	1.0 Tracta (Gregoire/Vallon)

1931

At long last: a potential home winner. Bugatti came in force and found no opposition from either the Bentley or the Mercedes factory. The British company was on the verge of liquidation and its colours, like those of its German rival, were flown by a solitary private entry. Indeed, two of the 'Bentley Boys' had moved to the Alfa Romeo camp, which represented Bugatti's biggest threat.

The new Alfa Romeo 8C 2300 (8-cylinder 2.3 litre) supercharged sports car proved so fast in practice that Bugatti decided to change pistons to raise the compression ratio of his unblown 4.9 litre cars, thereby allowing the use of pure benzene. Ettore Bugatti was renowned as an excellent innovative engineer and his sports/racing cars of the Twenties had notched up well over 2,000 wins. However, by the end of the decade it had become clear that his s.o.h.c. four- and eight-cylinder engines had reached the end of useful competition service.

1930 saw the launch of the 4.9 litre Type 50, of which the d.o.h.c. head was reminiscent of the two valves/cylinder American Miller Grand Prix car (of which Bugatti was known to have acquired two examples). Other than for its Miller-type head, the new straight-eight was traditional and at Le Mans it was hard pressed to match the power and road holding of the latest 150 b.h.p. Alfa Romeo.

With the more powerful Bentley and Mercedes in private hands, the works-assisted Alfa Romeo force set the standard in 1931. It had appeared to Alfa Romeo that the 6C had been, in all respects other than engine power, a more effective Le Mans car than the Bentley or Mercedes. The 6C had enjoyed a better power:weight ratio, better cornering ability, better braking and more effective streamlining. Encouraged by the Mussolini regime, Engineer Vittorio Jano had produced an engine which went a long way towards overcoming the only handicap...

Designed for Grand Prix racing, Jano's new straight-eight was of a twin block design – a crankshaft for each bank of four cylinders drove a central gear train from which a vertical shaft drove the d.o.h.c.s and the supercharger. This layout made for a very rigid bottom end. The cylinder dimensions were similar to those of the 6C and blown by a Roots supercharger the dry sump, 33.3% larger (2336cc) unit produced a lively 153 b.h.p. – over 66 b.h.p. per litre – at 5200 r.p.m. Fed through a four-speed gearbox, the straight-eight propelled a (Grand Prix influenced) 6C chassis with long, 3149mm, wheelbase for Le Mans. Even with mandatory

four-seater body the car weighed in at under 1000kgs. Top speed exceeded 110 m.p.h.

The 8C had made a disappointing debut on the Mille Miglia but had won the Targa Florio the following month and two were entered for Le Mans (Howe/Birkin and Zehender/Marinoni) with the aim of keeping Italian racing red to the fore.

Curiously painted black, the rival Bugattis not only lacked equal road holding but rejected treads in practice. National pride saw the home team stay with the troublesome Michelin tyres for the race. Alas, that was a fateful decision. A 6.30 p.m. Rost's Type 50 threw a tread which wrapped around the brake drum, pitching the car off the road. Rost and several marshals were injured and a spectator who had slipped into a prohibited area was killed. The Chiron/Varzi Type 50 had already lost treads without such dire consequences but when it threw a third, Team Manager Jean Bugatti, with great sadness, withdrew both remaining cars.

The loss of the three Bugattis left the race in Italian hands. The game Mercedes of Ivanowski/Stoffel had taken a share of the glory in the early stages but it, too, had suffered tyre troubles, eventually overcome through a switch from Engelburt to Dunlop tyres. By midnight the two Alfa Romeos were firmly in the lead. Distracted at Indianapolis, Zehender crashed: Howe/Birkin's Sunday drive became a straight-forward affair. A demonstration of the effectiveness of the new challenger – the British crew became the first to exceed 3000kms, albeit by a mere 17kms.

The Mercedes came away with fastest lap, slower than Birkin's record, but failed to worry Birkin and Howe en route to second spot. The private Bentley (Bevan/Cooper) fell by the wayside, as did a privately entered 5.3 litre Stutz and privately entered 6.3 and 4.3 litre Chryslers, the American

28

The Iwanowski/Stoffel Mercedes was the largest capacity car in the 1931 race and took a share of the glory in the early stages. However, like the favoured works Bugatti's, its challenge was blunted by tyre problems, leaving the race in Alfa Romeo hands. The winning Howe/Birkin 8C 2300 is the car in pursuit of the German hope. Photo: Autocar/Quadrant.

cars falling by the wayside before nightfall. However, a venerable La Lorraine was coaxed home in fourth place, behind the survivor of a two-car Talbot team.

Fox and Nichols had enlarged the Talbot six to 3.0 litres, from which it produced over 130 b.h.p. It had already taken the 3.0 litre honours in the Brooklands Double 12 event.

The widespread attrition of the more powerful cars was matched by that of the up to 3.0 litres (unblown) runners, of which only a 1500cc Aston Martin and a 1100cc Caban were classified, to make a sparse total of six finishers. The absence of factory teams (Bugatti's was the only full factory effort) had been sorely felt. However, the performance of the agile Alfa Romeo marked a turning point. 'The fastest lorry in the world' had given its place of honour to a new breed of lightweight, Grand Prix-bred sports car. Could Bugatti rise to Jano's innovation?

1.	2.3 Alfa Romeo* (Howe/Birkin)	4.	3.5 La Lorraine (Trebor/Balart)
2.	7.1 Mercedes-Benz* (Ivanowski/Stoffel)	5.	1.5 Aston Martin* (Cook/Bezzant)
3.	3.0 Talbot (Saunders/Davis/Rose-Richards)	6.	1.1 Caban* (Vernet/Vallon)
			* Class winners.

1932

In 1932 it was the turn of Sommer and Chinetti to win Le Mans for Alfa Romeo, the marque that was now dominating proceedings. Photo: Autocar/Quadrant.

The revised 8.38-mile circuit was the venue for a six-car Alfa Romeo onslaught. Bugatti offered two cars in opposition, powered by the supercharged 2.3 litre Grand Prix engine it had developed in 1931, but these Type 55s weren't fast enough. It was a three-car fight from the start and it was all Alfa: Marinoni's private 8C 2300 versus the two similar works cars in the hands of Minoia and Cortese.

During the second hour Marinoni, after breaking the lap record, went off and lost an hour. Then, at around 6.00 p.m., Minoia stole the lap record, only to take Maison Blanche too fast and hit a stricken blower Bentley. This sole example of the marque had been entered by two French amateurs and had crashed on the first lap. A solitary private Stutz had been quick to join the carnage: the Bentley and the Stutz had been two of only three over 3.0 litre cars – the third was a French-entered Mercedes which likewise crashed before nightfall.

As night drew in the Cortese/Guidotti works 8C 2300 led the works-assisted 8C 2300 of Howe/Birkin and the private 8C 2300 of Sommer/Chinetti, these three untroubled red cars chased by the Bugattis of Chinon/Bouriat and Czaikowski/Frederich. Trying hard to regain ground, Marinoni had joined the Maison Blanche wreckage.

Overnight Sommer/Chinetti and Howe/Birkin took turns at leading but at 3.00 a.m. the head gasket failed on the '31 winning car. The French and American crewed machine was left to plug on towards victory while Cortese/Guidotti attended to a number of parts working loose.

Both Bugatti Type 55s broke, Czaikowski/Frederich losing third place at noon, giving the Fox-Nichols Talbot team another splendid result. Its lone entry for Lewis/Rose-Richards lapsed onto five cylinders but managed to keep the 1750 (cc) Alfa Romeo of Siko/Sabipa in fourth place. Bugatti lost not only its supercharged hopes but also the 1500cc class to Aston Martin, which brought its small-engined runners home fifth and seventh.

Britain might have had some cheer thanks to the performance of its Talbot and Aston Martin runners, but the French 24-hour race was now firmly in the grip of the Italians. With Alfa Romeo hogging the limelight in Grand Prix racing, that situation could be expected to continue...

1.	2.3 Alfa Romeo* (Sommer/Chinetti)	5.	1.5 Aston Martin* (Newsome/Widengren)
2.	2.3 Alfa Romeo (Cortese/Guidotti)	6.	1.5 Bugatti (Sebilleau/Delaroche)
3.	3.0 Talbot (Lewis/Rose-Richards)		* Class winners. Also:
4.	1.8 Alfa Romeo* (Siko/Sabipa)	8.	1.1 Amilcar (Martin/Bodoignet)

1933

Alfa Romeo had suffered financially to the extent that it had come under the control of the state, which had closed its racing department. Much of the competition wing's equipment and many of its personnel had re-emerged in Modena under the banner of Enzo Ferrari's Scuderia Ferrari. There were again five 8C 2300s at Le Mans, including two new short wheelbase versions, dubbed 'Mille Miglias' following success in that event in '32 and '33. In contrast, Bugatti was represented by only one privately entered car, an old Type 50.

Aside from the Italian cars, the big capacity entry was paltry. Prince Nicolas of Rumania created some interest by entering a Model J Duesenberg – a big, heavy car with 6800cc, 32-valve 8-cylinder engine producing over 250 b.h.p. Popular with European royalty, the American car was too cumbersome for serious racing and, sadly, Nicolas's example was disqualified early on for refuelling too soon.

The blower Bentley and ancient La Lorraine re-appeared but both fell by the wayside, as did the old Bugatti. In any case, none of these amateur efforts had the measure of the Ferrari-fettled 8C 2300s.

The Mille Miglia of Nuvolari/Sommer set the pace – flat out – chased by the similar chassis of Chiron/Cortese, then the long wheelbase models of Chinetti/Varent and Lewis/Rose-Richards. The fifth car of Moll/Cloitre fell back under cover of darkness with failing lights, eventually having to call it a day.

Nuvolari/Sommer fell to third at half distance, a leaking fuel tank and broken front wing costing a quarter of an hour. But that sort of deficit didn't demoralize the Great Nuvolari...

At 10.00 a.m. the four-car Alfa Romeo procession became a three-car one, Cortese rolling spectacularly at the Esses. Thankfully, he suffered less than his car. Meanwhile, having set a new lap record, Nuvolari/Sommer were once more in the lead – but the battle was by no means over. The fuel tank leak continued to bug the leading duo, to the extent that they went into the last hour with but a two-minute advantage over Chinetti/Varent...

Through the last hour the lead see-sawed. The final drama appeared to have been enacted at 3.53 p.m. when Chinetti once more overtook Nuvolari's car as it was stationary in the pits. But the ace wasn't beaten yet – he roared off and caught Chinetti. The lead changed three times on the last lap. The inspired Chinetti was holding it when he overdid things at

Arnage, missing a gear and running out of road. Having broken the lap record nine times, Nuvolari won by 10 seconds...

Behind the three surviving 8C 2300s came a quartet of small capacity British cars. An 1800cc S.A.R.A. retired, a 1750 Alfa Romeo was lost in a fiery crash and a similar coupé-bodied car could finish no better than eighth, behind the British small fry.

Most successful of the English lightweights was the survivor of a new, two-car Riley team – one of its 1100cc cars had been an early retirement but the other beat both surviving 1500cc Aston Martins, which were split by a 750cc MG.

It was the same old story – Italians up front, Britons foremost among the classes. Was there room for the sought-after French revival?

1.	2.3 Alfa Romeo*	5.	1.5 Aston Martin*
	(Sommer/Nuvolari)		(Driscoll/Penn-Hughes)
2.	2.3 Alfa Romeo	6.	0.7 MG*
	(Chinetti/Varent)		(Ford/Baumer)
3.	2.3 Alfa Romeo		* Class winners. Also:
	(Lewis/Rose-Richards)	8.	1.8 Alfa Romeo
4.	1.1 Riley*		(Paco/Rousseau)
	(Peacock/van der Becke)		

1934

The field was growing – it exceeded 30 cars for the first time since 1928 with a total of 44 runners – but only a quarter of the entry boasted a capacity greater than 1500cc. While the lightweights were dominated numerically by British entries, the fight for overall honours came in the form of four Alfa Romeos and mixed bag of seven French machines with no hope on speed.

... But Sommer's Alfa Romeo lasted less than two hours. Having led the opening phase it burst into flames exiting Arnage. Then, while Howe/Rose-Richards held sway from Chinetti/Etancelin, the Saunders/Clifford example fell by the wayside. And when the lights went on the leading British crew found illumination problems, losing one hour. The old Type 50 Bugatti of Veyron/Labric, appropriately described by one French writer as like an elephant chasing gazelles, found itself with just one of the fleet red cars (four laps) ahead.

The elephant rather than the gazelle tripped up. Soon after midnight Bugatti's hope was shot. Two Type 55s had earlier fallen by the wayside (one due to mechanical failure, the other to disqualification) and a remaining Type 57 was not competitive. A 3.2 litre unblown, d.o.h.c.-engined car, this was a fast tourer rather than a racing car. Neither was the ageing La Lorraine in the hunt, and two unblown 2.0 litre V8 runners from the French Derby concern had joined the dead car park.

The eventual demise of all the over 1600cc French runners and the retirement of the delayed Howe/Rose-Richards' 2300cc before dawn due to a broken clutch, left second place overall as the reward for the most successful flyweight. The honour was disputed by Aston Martin and Riley. The Aston Martins broke and Riley claimed second, third, fifth and sixth positions, split by an 1100cc MG. A great day for the British marque – and another milestone for Alfa Romeo: a post-1927 record of four wins. It was now only one victory behind Bentley's claim to five successes...

1.	2.3 Alfa Romeo* (Chinetti/Etancelin)	4.	1.1 MG* (Martin/Eccles)
2.	1.5 Riley* (Sebilleau/Delaroche)	5.	1.1 Riley (Peacock/van der Becke)
3.	1.5 Riley (Dixon/Paul)	6.	1.1 Riley (Newsome/MacLure)
			* Class winners.

1935

The quality, at least at the front of the field, was thin, but at least the quantity was still there. In Grand Prix racing Alfa Romeo and Bugatti's early Thirties designs had been completely outclassed by new Mercedes and Auto Union cars. At Le Mans the solid 8C 2300 was still competitive and the faithful Veyron/Labric Type 50 could still give it a run for its money. But at least there was another challenger to the ageing elephant and not-so-young gazelles – one in the idiom of the former.

Arthur Fox's Fox and Nichols' team had switched its allegiance from Talbot back to Lagonda, attracted to the competition potential of the M45 fast tourer. Unveiled in 1933 and uprated to M45R – Rapide – specification in 1934, this was a conventional Thirties sporting car (with semi-elliptic sprung ladder frame chassis) propelled by a 4.5 litre straight-six Meadows engine. Although a push rod design of the Twenties, B. S. Crump's six had good tuning potential: Fox and Nichols managed to extract 150 b.h.p. The team entered a three-car squad for the 1934 Ards T.T. and, encouraged by fourth, fifth and eighth places, dispatched two of the cars to Le Mans in 1935.

Right from the start the Lagondas of Hindmarsh/Fontes and Benjafield/Gunter were on the pace of the four supercharged Alfa Romeos, driven by Lewis/Howe (who led for the first six laps before requiring a distributor change), Sommer/de Sauge, Stoffel/Louis-Dreyfus and Chinetti/Gastard (who took over on lap seven and led until needing a wheel change at the end of the first hour). The 4.9 litre Bugatti was in there, too.

Throughout a rainy evening and wet night the Alfas and the Lagonda of Hindmarsh/Fontes took turns at leading, the latter inheriting first place when Sommer, driving solo as his co-driver had been taken ill, was delayed seven laps by a blocked fuel line. The Lagonda, leading at midnight, had the Howe/Lewis and Stoffel/Dreyfus Alfas and the Bugatti on the same lap.

The Lagonda of Hindmarsh/Fontes was the somewhat surprising winner of the 1935 24-hour race, the sturdy British Racing Green car ending a long run by the fleet red machines from Italy. Photo: Autocar/Quadrant.

Sunday morning saw more mechanical ailments – Sommer's 8C 2300 retired, then the Bugatti broke its back axle. The tide was turning in Lagonda's favour and subsequently Chinetti/Gaston retired after two off-road excursions and Howe/Lewis lost a piston. By midday Hindmarsh/Fontes had pulled a comfortable margin over Dreyfus/Stoffel. Although the second Lagonda was falling back with gearbox bothers, it seemed that nothing now would stop a British win. However, during the 24th hour Fontes started making frequent stops due to falling oil pressure. Dreyfus passed the car as it sat in its pit. Signalled that he was in the lead, he backed off – to lose by five minutes thanks to a lap scoring error by his team! Although stuck in top, the second Lagonda came home 13th, to give the British marque a 100% finishing record.

Of the 28 finishers, 22 were British cars. This year no less than 36 small cars had swarmed across the channel (out of a record entry of 58 cars, 40 were of 1500cc or less) and high places went to Aston Martin (third, despite the loss of all but top gear) and Riley (fourth).

While Le Mans seemed increasingly a British race on French soil, there was little joy for the home runners, which included unsuccessful private entries of one Type 57 and two Type 55 Bugattis and the old La Lorraine. However, there was a glimmer of hope in the arrival of two new marques: Automobiles Talbot and Delahaye/Delage.

The French Talbot company had been taken over (and given new independence) by competition enthusiast Antonio Lago, a French domiciled Venetian, while Delahaye had absorbed Delage, the foremost French racing car constructor prior to 1928. Talbot had yet to unveil its planned sporting/competition sports car but made an (unsuccessful) trial run with an old 3.0 litre coupé. Delahaye ran its first sporting car, a 1934-launched Jean Françoise-designed machine boasting independent front suspension by transverse leaf spring and robust 3.2 litre six-cylinder push rod engine. Awaiting more power, this marque's exploratory outing netted fifth place.

Bugatti might have shown little interest in Le Mans since the early Thirties but there was still hope of a French revival. And there was still that great amateur sporting spirit: Prince Nicholas of Rumania hadn't given up, despite disqualification in '33 and a seized engine in practice in '34. His giant 6.8 litre Duesenberg had once more headed the line-up... only to retire on Saturday evening. But bigger unblown engines were once more in vogue and both Delahaye and Talbot had ideas in this direction...

1.	4.5 Lagonda* (Hindmarsh/Fontes)	5.	3.2 Delahaye (Paris/Mongin)
2.	2.3 Alfa Romeo* (Dreyfus/Stoffel)	6.	1.8 Alfa Romeo* (Desvignes/Don)
3.	1.5 Aston Martin* (Martin/Brackenbury)		* Class winners. Also:
4.	1.5 Riley (Richardson/van der Becke)	9.	1.1 MG (Maillard/Brune-Druck)
		27.	0.7 Austin (Carr/Barbour)

1937

Home runners Talbot and Delahaye/Delage were prominent among the potential winners. In the light of the German state-backed Grand Prix onslaught, France had focused her attention firmly upon sports car racing – even the 1936 French Grand Prix was for sports cars. That was the encouragement the revitalized French marques had responded to.

Talbot designer Walter Becchia had penned an intriguing pent roof head with overhead valves operated by cross pushrods. This was mated to an existing, rugged straight six block to produce a 4.0 litre engine capable of a reliable 160 b.h.p. That power was transmitted through a four-speed Wilson preselector gearbox. Becchia produced a suitable open cockpit racing chassis with independent front suspension using transverse leaf spring and semi-elliptic rear suspension. The potential of the new 'Talbot-Lago' was sufficient to attract Scuderia Ferrari Grand Prix driver Dreyfus to the marque as Team Manager and lead driver.

For its part, Delahaye had developed a larger bore version of its straight-six breathing through three twin-choke carburettors. The rejuvenated 3.6 litre engine endowed its 135M competition sports car with 160 b.h.p. at 4200 r.p.m. That was fed through a Cotal epicyclic gearbox in which each gear was engaged by electro-magnetic clutches. The marque collected second, third, fourth and fifth places in the 1936 French Grand Prix... beaten by Bugatti.

With its Grand Prix cars outmoded and the flourishing of sports car racing in its native land, the Molsheim marque had jumped onto the band wagon. 1936 was a year of strife for the concern, during which Ettore Bugatti got locked out of his own factory. He moved to Paris and son Jean, creator of the new competition sports car, took over. It was also a year of strife for the nation as a whole – civil unrest caused the late cancellation of the Le Mans race. Bugatti hadn't entered in any case, but it was ready with two of its French Grand Prix winning 'Tanks' for the '37 event...

The so-called 'Tank' was a competition version of the 3.2 litre Type 57 with shorter, stiffer, lower frame, split axle front suspension and a dry sump version of the d.o.h.c. straight-eight coaxed to produce in excess of 170 b.h.p. Its nickname came from the clothing Jean Bugatti devised for it – a bulbous open body, designed for low drag, with the wings fared in as part of the wide, all-enveloping beetle-shape main shell.

By 1937 France had the equipment to win her own classic motor race once more. The victorious Bugatti of Benoist/Wimille was dubbed a 'Tank' and demonstrated bullet-proof reliability. Photo: Autocar/Quadrant.

37

One of the Type 57 G 'Tanks' was entrusted to Type 50 stalwarts Veyron/Labric, while Benoist/Wimille shared the actual Grand Prix winning example. The opposition included no less than seven Delahayes (including private entries), two Talbots and a Delahaye-built 'Delage', a new D6/70 design with 140 b.h.p. six-cylinder engine of 2.7 litres. The other big capacity runners were two (traditionally clothed) Bugattis (of 3.2 and 3.0 litres), an Alfa Romeo in the hands of Sommer/Guidotti and a Lagonda ... only two non-French cars among 16 over 2.0 litre runners this year.

The Alfa Romeo was a fiercesome beast, with 2.9 litre supercharged engine inherited from the marque's mid-Thirties' Grand Prix car, essentially a big capacity version of the regular split crank eight. Its power output was around 200 b.h.p. and its Grand Prix-derived chassis was all independently sprung, with trailing links and coil springs at the front and transverse leaf spring at the rear.

The Lagonda was another improved car. The marque had acquired the services of W. O. Bentley following its 1935 Le Mans win and he provided the basis for a faster Fox and Nichols racer. Alas, both the Alfa Romeo and the Lagonda were early casualties, leaving the overall honours a French fight for a change.

But not before Sommer had shown the potential of the bigger capacity 8C 2900A, leading the first four laps. By no means did he have an advantage, though: Wimille took over on lap five, having broken the lap record as he recovered from a slow start, he proceeded to pull away.

Alas, no sooner was the race shaping up as an intriguing contest between the lone Italian car and the French horde than a tragic accident blackened the proceedings. Kippeurt lost control of his old Bugatti and a subsequent six-car pile up claimed his life and that of Fraser Nash driver Fairfield (the first drivers killed since 1925) and removed a Talbot and a Delahaye from the proceedings. The retirement of the Alfa Romeo on the very next lap left Wimille/Benoist comfortably to outrun the rest of the field. The Veyron/Labric sister car, however, lost a safe third place on Sunday morning due to a split fuel tank. Their misfortune left second, third and fourth places to the Delahaye/Delage company, the unique Delage taking fourth.

There were only four healthy examples of the 14 big French cars at the end. However, the winning Bugatti had become the first car to exceed 2,000 miles in 24 hours. A 1500cc Aston Martin took fifth place – the English contingent could still shrug off any foreign small capacity opposition but now the race for overall honours was very much in French hands.

1.	3.3 Bugatti* (Wimille/Benoist)	5.	1.5 Aston Martin* (Skeffington/Murton-Neale)
2.	3.6 Delahaye (Paul/Mongin)	6.	1.7 Adler* (Orssich/Sauerwein)
3.	3.6 Delahaye (Dreyfus/Stoffel)		* Class winners. Also:
4.	3.0 Delage* (de Valence/Gerard)	12.	1.0 Simca (Vernet/Largeot)
		17.	0.6 Simca (Viale/Alin)

1938

Once again the French Grand Prix cast an influence upon the Le Mans entry list. After two years of encouragement for the development of the French sports-racing car it reverted to the international Grand Prix formula, 3.0 litres supercharged, 4.5 litres unblown. Both Talbot and Delahaye/Delage produced Grand Prix cars. Talbot developed a 4.5 litre version of its straight-six and entered Grand Prix races with a stripped sports car. Delahaye produced a proper Grand Prix contender with purpose-designed 4.5 litre V12 engine. Both concerns used their Grand Prix motors for faster Le Mans cars.

The 12-cylinder unit designed for the Delahaye *monoplace* featured two plugs per cylinder and a total of three camshafts – both banks shared a common inlet shaft located within the vee. It produced over 200 b.h.p. but that was no match for the rival German Grand Prix cars. However, it was economical.

Delahaye also developed an improved Le Mans chassis with semi-elliptic rear end the only major departure from the contemporary single seater. It was essentially a Grand Prix car with widened body, second seat (only two were now called for), cycle wings and lighting equipment. Two were entered by Laury and Lucy Shell's 'Ecurie Bleue', to be driven by Chiron/Dreyfus and Comotti/Divo. Talbot replied with a single 4.5-litre car for Etancelin/Chinetti.

Behind the new 4.5 litre French cars were a host of smaller capacity Talbots and Delahaye/Delages, as seen in '37, plus a fourth car capable of producing over 200 b.h.p. – the latest Alfa Romeo 8C 2900B for Sommer/Biondetti. Alfa Romeo had opened new competition wing *Alfa Corse* and, whereas the French were running 4.5 litre open cockpit specials, it had commissioned a fully enclosed, coupé body, with strikingly long nose ahead of a stubby two-seater cockpit, from Touring of Milan. The base car, the 8C 2900B, was one of the world's fastest catalogued production cars with a claimed top speed close on 140 m.p.h., but only a handful of 8C 2900 models had been built.

The performance of the twin Roots blower equipped 2.9 litre Alfa Romeo engine was again adequate. Sommer made a poor start but was soon mixing with the 4.5 litre French cars at Grand Prix-like pace. After only seven laps a bolt found its way into the gearbox of the Comotti-driven Delahaye, reducing the scrap to a three-way one: Sommer versus Dreyfus versus Etancelin.

The pace proved too hot for the new Delahaye engine – after 23 laps Dreyfus came in with overheating. Another lap had to be completed before water could be taken on. That lap reduced the V12 to junk. So it was that as night drew in only the Etancelin/Chinetti Talbot was left to worry Sommer/Biondetti. And before long that threat had gone, too. At 9.00 p.m. the Talbot was pushed away with a broken valve.

The demise of the 4.5 litre runners left the Le Begue/Carrierc 4.0-litre Talbot well behind the fleeing Alfa Romeo. It broke its gearbox, leaving the sister cars of Trevoux/Levegh and Mathieson/Clifford respectively five and eight laps in arrears as Sunday morning started to unfold. But those cars also failed, the former due to head gasket failure, the latter to a fire. First light revealed Sommer/Biondetti close on 10 laps and still drawing away, from the Delahayes of Chaboud/Tremoulet and Serraud/Giraud-Cabantous. These were familiar 135 Competition models, of which two of five had fallen by the wayside. A lone 2.7 litre Delage had likewise come to grief.

By Sunday afternoon the Alfa Romeo had a 13-lap advantage, despite a burst tyre which had punched a hole in the wing. That had been patched up... only for the car to drop a valve. The surprised Chabout/Tremoulet found themselves en route for victory. Another great home win!

Behind the memorable Delahaye one-two was the survivor of the five-strong 4.0 litre Talbot ranks (Prenant/Morel) and the fifth Delahaye 135 (Villeneuve/Biolay). An older 2.6 litre Alfa Romeo fell by the wayside, as did a 2.5 litre Amilcar, and fifth place was taken by the sole survivor of a three-strong Darl'Mat Peugeot team, which collected the 2.0 litre honours. It was followed home by a 1.7 litre and a 1.5 litre Adler, these aerodynamic German coupés running regularly and reliably to complete the overthrow of the British rule of the small capacity classes.

Even without Bugatti, France was continuing her new-found rule of the overall honours... with the help of a little luck. The Molsheim marque had tested a supercharged Tank, but had decreed it not yet ready to race. There could be an even faster French challenge the following year...

1.	3.6 Delahaye* (Chaboud/Tremoulet)	6.	1.7 Adler (Orssich/Sauerwein)
2.	3.6 Delahaye (Serraud/Giraud-Cabantous)		* Class winners. Also:
		7.	1.5 Adler (Lohr/von Guilleaume)
3.	4.0 Talbot (Prenant/Morel)	8.	1.0 Singer (Savoye/Savoye)
4.	3.6 Delahaye (Villeneuve/Boilay)	14.	0.6 Simca (Aime/Plantivaux)
5.	2.0 Peugeot-Darl'mat* (de Cortanze/Contet)		

1939

The Bugatti Tank was back, now a 150 m.p.h. car thanks to a Roots supercharger. But it played a game of caution. So did the other favourites. Delahaye abandoned its V12 engine in favour of the trusty 135 Competition, of which there were eight examples, plus a pair of D6/70 Delages. Chinetti entered three 4.5 litre Talbots, while three 4.0 litres were in private hands. Sommer plumped for a new 150 b.h.p. six-cylinder d.o.h.c. Alfa Romeo – the coupé-bodied 6C 2500, of the type that had won the gruelling Mille Miglia. Driven up from the Milan factory, it only just made the scrutineering deadline.

The new Italian car proved no more reliable than the fast, highly stressed 8C 2900s that had failed Sommer in '37 and '38. Early plug problems were followed by a change of head gasket, which took an hour. And still the car didn't see the finish...

While the works Bugatti in the hands of Wimille/Veyron ran regularly, the fastest Delahaye, Delage and Talbot representatives headed the field. The battle was between the Delahaye of Mazaud/ Mongin, the Delage of Gerard/Monneret and, as darkness fell, the Talbot of Chinetti/Mathieson.

First to go was the Delahaye. At 2.00 a.m. it caught fire and burned out in front of the pits. Much later on Sunday morning the Talbot went into the sand. Mathieson got it back onto the road, only for its engine to give up the ghost. The Delage, which had done much of the pace-making overnight, looked sure to win. But then its day turned sour – a valve spring broke. Gerard/Monneret could but limp home behind Wimille/ Veryon...

For the others of the 17 big French cars there was no joy. The first Delahaye home was a troubled sixth, behind a 2.0 litre BMW, while none of the Talbots finished. Third and fourth places fell to Lagonda, making its return with a full works team.

In 1937 the 4.5 litre, six-cylinder Meadows-engined Lagonda had been replaced by a new car powered by a W. O. Bentley-designed V12 of the same capacity. It was intended as a luxury tourer and featured independent front suspension. A late decision was made to enter two lightened and suitably modified examples for the '39 race, by way of a trial run. So a Bentley engine with the potential to win was back. But W.O. didn't want to run it and the two cars (Dobson/Brackenbury and Selsdon/Waleran) were paced very carefully. True, Dobson took the lead at the start, but by the end of the first lap he was second (having been demoted by Chinetti), by the end of the second lap he was sixth and it wasn't until the French ranks became decimated that the hurriedly prepared, gently driven British cars again appeared high in the order.

Behind the clockwork Lagondas (which ran throughout on one set of tyres), were three impressive 2.0 litre K.N.C.C.-entered BMWs, which took fifth, seventh and ninth to dominate the small car ranks. Adler had moved up to 2.5 litres with just one entry, which was an early retirement with a broken piston. Nevertheless, Germany was giving France something to think about...

1.	3.3 Bugatti*	6. 3.6 Delahaye
	(Wimille/Veyron)	(Villeneuve/Boilay)
2.	3.0 Delage*	* Class winners. Also:
	(Gerard/Monneret)	10. 1.1 Simca
3.	4.5 Lagonda	(Gordini/Scaron)
	(Dobson/Brackenbury)	14. 1.5 HRG
4.	4.5 Lagonda	(Clark/Chambers)
	(Selsdon/Waleran)	19. 0.6 Simca
5.	2.0 BMW*	(Alin/Alin)
	(Wenscher/von Schaumburg-Lippe)	

Part Two
1949 - 86

1949

Enzo Ferrari could count himself relatively lucky. During the war contract work had kept his Modena-based engineering concern on a sound financial footing. A one-time Alfa Romeo racing driver-cum-manager, he had branched out on his own at the end of the Twenties and his team had run the Alfa Romeo race programme until 1938. When Ferrari had split with the Milan marque he had agreed not to produce rival machines for at least four years. The Ferrari marque had to wait somewhat longer than that for its official baptism...

Former Alfa Romeo engineer Gioacchini Colombo began work on a V12 engine for Ferrari in 1946 and, supported by Ferrari's wealthy wife and a number of patrons, the marque began its illustrious racing career in May, 1947. Its first Tipo 125 sports car had a capacity of 1.5 litres but by 1949 the V12's displacement had been increased to 2.0 litres from which the 60 degree vee engine with single overhead camshaft per bank, breathing through three Webers, produced 140 b.h.p. (70 per litre). For late Forties sports car races it propelled a light, rugged tubular frame, two-seater chassis with independent front suspension by transverse leaf spring and a semi-elliptic sprung independent rear end. The '166' was either coupé-bodied or, in sports-racing 'MM' guise, carried a light open cockpit *barchetta* body by Touring of Milan which, in novel fashion, was based around a cage of small diameter tubing.

Campaigned by customers, in 1948 the 166 won both Italian sports car classics, the Targa Florio and the Mille Miglia. And in 1949 it did it again. That year Scuderia Ferrari re-emerged as a full-scale racing team with designs on Formula Two and Grand Prix racing as well as the sports car classics. With open wheel bodywork the 166 proved very competitive in 1949 Formula Two races.

By 1949 the ACO had revived its 24-hour fixture and two *barchetta* 166s were entered, one to be driven by Chinetti who, the previous September, had won the Paris 12-hours at Montlhery single-handed, defeating 3.6 litre Delahayes and 4.5 litre Talbots with his little, light 2.0 litre car. With good power and an excellent power-to-weight ratio, the diminutive Italian V12-propelled machine was clearly something to be respected.

Sadly, the Circuit de la Sarthe hadn't come out of the war as well as the fledgling Italian marque. Having housed a Luftwaffe base, it had suffered extensive bombing and what remained had been destroyed by retreating Germans. Nevertheless, having taken the decision to revive the twice-around-the-clock classic in 1948, the ACO had reconstructed the track by June, 1949. Its fast layout remained largely unaltered and at the revival event would be pounded by no less than 29 French cars, including three Talbots, seven Delahayes and four Delages of familiar pre-war type. The French flocked to witness another great home win.

Sure enough, the old French warriors set the early pace – but the new Italian lightweights were with the heavy metal. And when Chaboud's leading Delahaye caught fire and was retired after four-and-a-half hours, the Ferraris moved ahead . . .

Just after 9.00 p.m., Dreyfus/Lucas' surprising little red car crashed into retirement. Chinetti's partner, Lord Selsdon, had been taken ill but overnight the remaining 2.0 litre warrior (in which a higher r.p.m. needle roller bearing engine had not proved an advantage) moved into a firm lead, aided by the retirement of two more of the faster French cars. That lead was preserved right to the end, although a slipping clutch allowed the Louveau/Jover Delage to move to within one lap after 24 hours . . .

The win was a great personal triumph for Chinetti, who had driven 22 hours single handed, and was another feather in the cap of Ferrari, which was in the midst of a Formula Two winning streak. Within three years the marque had developed into a major force in motor racing. The Le Mans triumph did much for its image and helped revive the international reputation of the 24-hour race.

Of course, Ferrari was a small, specialist racing car constructor, not a major manufacturer like Talbot or Delahaye/Delage. One of the old big sixes (a Delahaye 135 Competition driven by Simon) salvaged fastest lap, a shade slower than the 96 m.p.h. '39 record set by a similar car, but all the grand marques could muster were class wins – the 3.0 litre honours to the second placed D63L (a development of the old D6/70) and the over 3.0 litre award to the Brunet/Grignard 135 which finished fifth.

The moral victor of that award was the 4.5 litre Talbot driven by Chambas/Morel. A private entry, Chambas had bought the car as a bare chassis and had equipped it with his own design of streamlined coupé coachwork. While both works Talbots retired, Chambas' special rumbled

After a ten-year interlude French enthusiasts came back to Le Mans to see another great victory for the big national sports cars, such as this Delage. It was not to be . . . Photo: LAT.

Surprise of the revived 1949 Le Mans race was this little 2.0 litre Ferrari, driven by Chinetti/Selsdon to a convincing win. Photo: LAT.

on, only to run out of fuel on the mandatory slowing down lap. The ACO credited the car with 59 seconds less than the 24 hours' duration and disqualified it, promoting another Delage to fourth, to the chagrin of Talbot.

An intriguing runner among the dozen big French cars (which also ran out of fuel) was a 4.4 litre Delettrez diesel car. On the whole the big French cars were unlucky and there was little for the locals to cheer. Third overall was a 2.0 litre Frazer Nash driven by Aldington and Culpan. Aston Martin lost the glory of that position due to a crash which claimed the life of works driver Marechal early on Sunday afternoon. The Fraser Nash had previously led the British contingent, until afflicted by a clutch problem.

Rounding out the top six was a glorious Bentley 'Experimental Streamliner' with over 60,000 miles on the clock. At the instigation of the marque's French importer this car had been equipped with its special coachwork, designed by a Parisian dentist. The importer, Sleator, had proved it capable of in excess of 120 m.p.h. with its straight-six tuned to supply something more than the standard 125 b.h.p. By 1949 it was in the hands of the Englishman Hay whose cruise home, accompanied by Wisdom, was only spoilt by a puncture and the loss of overdrive with two hours to go. The performance of the old British warrior emphasised how little progress had been made: its average speed was less than 75 m.p.h. Yet with a new breed of car emerging, the 100 m.p.h. lap was clearly going to become commonplace.

1.	2.0 Ferrari* (Chinetti/Selsdon)	6.	4.4 Bentley (Hay/Wisdom)
2.	3.0 Delage* (Louveau/Jover)		* Class winners. Also:
3.	2.0 Frazer Nash (Culpan/Aldington)	8.	1.5 HRG (Thompson/Fairman)
4.	3.0 Delage (Gerard-Fales)	12.	1.1 Monopole (de Montremy/Dussous)
5.	3.6 Delahaye* (Grignard/Brunet)	15.	0.7 Aero Minor (Kratmer/Sutner)

46

1950

With the track resurfaced and some corners widened or eased, the first 100 m.p.h. lap so nearly fell to Sommer in practice, the French veteran having postponed a planned retirement to drive a Ferrari (for ever championing the Italian cause!). This year there were five of the pretty little *barchettas*, two using bored-out 170 b.h.p. 2.3 litre V12 engines. Sommer's blue 2.3 litre '195S' was the swiftest, heading practice and the early laps. On lap 19 he backed up his sizzling practice form with an official lap record of 98.3 m.p.h. However, not long afterwards fellow Frenchman Rosier stole the 100 m.p.h. honour, wringing 102.84 m.p.h. out of his rather special Talbot while Sommer was changing a plug...

During the third hour Sommer, having regained the advantage, suffered a broken dynamo fixing bracket and the Talbot forged ahead. Later the fleet Ferrari retired with complete electrical failure – and all other examples of the young Italian marque were destined to retire, too. Chinetti's sister 195S, having held second place at midnight, two laps adrift of Rosier's Talbot, succumbed to a broken axle.

Once free of Sommer, Rosier had taken charge and the French motor industry got its revenge. But it was won by a somewhat controversial car. In the Thirties Antonio Lago's Grand Prix cars might have used converted sports car engines, but in the mood of post-war optimism he had been a little more ambitious. Inspired by victory for his pre-war car in the 1947 French Grand Prix, he and chief engineer Carlo Marchetti had hatched a proper Grand Prix Talbot with purpose-designed 4.5 litre d.o.h.c. straight-six.

The 240 b.h.p. (53 per litre) Lago Talbot's chassis was a sleeker, refined version of existing hardware (with ladder frame and semi-elliptic independent front suspension). The intention was that it should be a strong, reliable car for privateer use. Heavy and somewhat sluggish compared to the 1.5 litre supercharged opposition, it was best suited to longer races on circuits without too many sharp bends. In 1949 Lago Talbot won Grands Prix at Spa and Rheims.

In 1950 Alfa Romeo returned to Grand Prix racing and the Lago Talbot was completely overshadowed by the 1.5 litre blown 159. Leading Talbot driver Rosier turned his attention to Le Mans, fitting a widened body, second seat, cycle wings and lighting equipment and lowering the compression ratio in the interests of 24-hour reliability. He nominated his son to co-drive but hogged the limelight, going one better than Chinetti to complete all but 20 minutes of the run to victory.

Once Sommer's Ferrari had wilted, Rosier had no worry other than a broken rocker arm which cost 25 minutes and gave another works car in the hands of Meyrat/Mairesse a short-lived lead. This was a rebodied pre-war car and it came home a mere ten miles behind the exhausted Grand Prix driver's charge.

The only other Talbot in the race was the Chambas streamliner which this year completed 24 hours, taking 13th place – overshadowed as surely as the two Delahayes and lone Delage in the race. There were two other big capacity French cars, both with diesel engines – the familiar Delettrez and a radical MAP with centrally mounted 5.0 litre supercharged engine. Neither featured.

While the race was a triumph for France it was equally uplifting for Britain, which lost only two of 16 entries and scooped the top 10 placings behind the winning Talbots.

Leading what *Motor* magazine described as a 'British revival' was a Cadillac V8 engined special driven by constructor Sydney Allard. A practical rather than a scientific engineer, Allard had started building his own Ford-based cars before the war and soon after it had offered his first production machine, a trials car. Designed with American road racing in mind, his 5.4 litre V8-engined J2, which was making its Le Mans debut, featured a short, light two-seater chassis with split front axle and de Dion rear end and unaerodynamic open bodywork using cycle wings. Not sophisticated, but fast enough to run with the Talbots and Ferraris in the early stages.

At midnight, Allard/Cole held fourth place behind Rosier, Chinetti and Meyrat but after half distance they lost a lot of time with a gearbox problem and were left with only top from the three-speed unit. Nevertheless, the car recovered to claim third from the Rolt/Hamilton streamlined Nash Healey with less than one hour to go.

The Healey marque was the creation of competition driver and Triumph designer Donald Healey and had been founded, like Ferrari and Allard, in 1946. Its 3.8 litre Nash-engined two-seater was, like the Allard, aimed at the American market.

Behind the specials came the two survivors of a three-car works Aston Martin team. The familiar British marque had been saved from liquidation by David Brown, a tractor manufacturer who had snapped up the ailing Lagonda concern in the late Forties. The first car under Brown, the DB1 coupé, featured an advanced tubular spaceframe chassis with coil spring rear suspension. Launched in 1948, it was followed in 1950 by the DB2 coupé with shorter chassis and 2.6 litre d.o.h.c. six designed by W.O. for Lagonda. The 120 b.h.p. Le Mans-prepared DB2 of Abecassis/Macklin won the Index of Performance with its solid run to fifth place.

Misfortune had struck the team en route to the event. Travelling through France, one of the three 'LB6'-engined coupés had been crashed so a DB2 prototype seen in the '49 event had been brought back into service. Alas, it had only lasted eight laps, probably as it had been run for too long on warm-up plugs in practice. However, the other cars had run like trains to take the 3.0-litre honours.

48

Jaguar also had three lightly modified road cars in the race this year, although these were run by privateers. However, the entries were made with the full support of the factory and were managed by works Service Engineer 'Lofty' England. Although the marque was concentrating on saloon car production, the models in question were XK120 rag top sports cars. The new open top model had a 3.4 litre d.o.h.c. straight-six and a chassis with independent front suspension by wishbones and coil springs. With smooth, flowing lines, 160 b.h.p. engine and very modest price tag, the MK VII saloon-based sports car's looks and performance had caused a stir when it had been unveiled in 1948 and the excitement had been fuelled by an officially timed 123 m.p.h. run and victory in a 1949 Silverstone race to determine Britain's fastest production car.

For 1950 six near-standard aluminium-bodied cars were supplied to favoured privateers and three of these were entered for Le Mans. To the pleasant surprise of the company the XK120 of Johnson/Hadley ran well up the field and at noon was leading the pursuit of the Talbots, despite brake bothers. When it retired at 1.00 p.m., it was actually lapping faster than the leading car...

Jaguar had the consolations of finishes (12th and 15th) for its other cars, neither of which was in the best of health, and of knowing that it had the basis of a Le Mans winner...

... Even if it had finished behind a 1934 Bentley – a TT car and one of two examples of the great British marque. The other was the Experimental Streamliner, which managed a higher average speed this year yet languished in a lowly 14th position.

If the British fleet had given the French plenty to think about, so too had two entries from the USA. American sportsman Briggs Cunningham had organised a team of Series 61 Cadillac sedans. One ran with a standard coupé body, the other with experimental open body devised by the aircraft manufacturer Grumman. It was as curvacious as a brick. The French called it 'Le Monstre' and dubbed the sister car 'Petite Patoud'...

Equipped with two-way pits – car radios, the 5.4 litre Frick-Tappet tuned machines rolled home 10th and 11th, Le Monstre cruising throughout Sunday with only top gear (thankfully only needing to stop every four hours to replenish its 50 gallon tank). For Cunningham, the race was an exploratory outing – albeit one that got off badly as he had to dig Le Monstre out of a sandbank soon after the start. He was destined to play an important role in the future of the event. So too were Aston Martin and Jaguar.

1.	4.5 Talbot* (Rosier/Rosier)	6.	2.6 Aston Martin (Parnell/Brackenbury)
2.	4.5 Talbot (Meyrat/Mairesse)		* Class winners. Also:
3.	5.4 Allard* (Allard/Cole)	9.	2.0 Frazer-Nash (Stoop/Mathieson)
4.	3.8 Healey (Rolt/Hamilton)	16.	1.5 Jowett (Wisdom/Wise)
5.	2.6 Aston Martin* (Macklin/Abecassis)	21.	0.7 Aero Minor (Gatsonides/Hoogeveen)
		24.	0.8 Renault (Sandt/Coatalen)

1951

Observing the performance of the XK120s in the 1950 race, Jaguar Engineering Director William Heynes came to the conclusion that a lighter chassis equipped with XK running gear could win the race. Sir William Lyons gave the go ahead on the spot but it was winter before work commenced on the 'XK120C' due to pressure of other projects. Nevertheless, by May, 1951, the Jaguar Le Mans car was ready. The C-type, as it became known, had a tubular frame chassis with improved torsion bar suspension front and rear and better brakes. It was clad in an aerodynamically efficient aluminium shell and its XK engine was tuned to produce around 200 b.h.p. (59 b.h.p. per litre). Drivers were Moss/Fairman, Whitehead/Walker and Johnson/Biondetti.

The C-type's 3.4 litre capacity let a lot of cars ahead of it in the line-up but by the end of the first lap Moss had only Gonzales' 4.5 litre Talbot in front. Quickly the British boy in the British car took command. Driving carefully, yet pulling away, Jaguar's 'hare' set a new lap record of 105.2 m.p.h. on lap 31. Within two hours Moss had lapped the entire field.

As evening drew in the C-types were one-two-three, the more conservatively run cars hounded by the faster Talbots and Ferraris. But at 8.30 p.m. there was consternation in the Jaguar pit. Johnson/Biondetti had suffered a broken oil pipe flange – and the problem could just as easily strike the other cars. Sure enough, Moss/Fairman lost oil pressure and broke a con rod. However, for Whitehead/Walker it was the opposition rather than the car which weakened and they continued to run at a comfortable pace to win by 67 miles.

Victory put Jaguar on the map as an internationally renowned motor manufacturer and left Talbot and Ferrari humbled. Talbot lost its two fastest works cars in the hands of Gonzales/Marimon and Rosier/Fangio to a burst radiator and engine failure, having shown the pace to match all but Jaguar's hare. Ferrari was also unable to reach that pace and had trouble with all its quick runners.

This year there was a 2.6 litre version of the familiar V12 sports car, the 212, but this was overshadowed by Ferrari's first big-engined sports car, the 'America' with Lampredi-designed V12.

The Lampredi engine was an all-new 60 degree s.o.h.c. V12, produced originally at 3.3 litres (72mm × 68mm). However, the bore had been taken out to 80mm to provide a 4.1 litre displacement from which the wet sump unit churned 280 b.h.p. (68.2 per litre). The 'America' sports-racing car had a gearbox integral with the engine, transverse leaf spring front suspension, semi-elliptic rear. The car was good enough to win the Mille Miglia but the four entered for Le Mans were overshadowed by the lighter, more aerodynamic and better handling Jaguar. Ferrari lacked chassis sophistication and stamina, only Chinetti/Lucas coaxing their troubled example home eighth. Clutch failure, starter failure and disqualification for premature refuelling took out the other examples. Two of three 212s finished, well down the order, as did a lone 166.

Talbot at least salvaged second for its last remaining works car in the hands of Meyrat/Mairesse, while the private entry of Levegh/Marchand finished fourth. This year Chambas' car had a new open body but managed no better than 17th position.

Still, it fared better than the three other big-engined French hopes, a Talbot, a lone Delahaye and the unique Delettrez diesel, all of which fell by the wayside.

To claim second and fourth positions, Talbot had to fight with Aston Martin which, unlike Jaguar, didn't yet have its purpose-built Le Mans car. The marque had put new Chief Engineer Professor Eberan von Eberhorst to work to produce a potential winning car based around its straight six, but this wouldn't be ready until later in the season. Team Manager Wyer therefore organised three lightweight DB2s (weighing 200kgs less than the '50 team cars) which, thanks to three twin-choke Webers and porting modifications, produced 140 b.h.p. They all went faster than the '50 class-winning average speed to come home first, second and third in the up to 3.0 litre division. Macklin/Thompson drove the second half of the race flat out and finished only six miles behind the second placed Talbot, while the other cars finished fifth and seventh, split by the 3.0 litre Nash Healey. That car featured a more bulbous streamlined body and failed by mere seconds to beat the fifth placed Aston Martin...

Private DB2s came home 10th and 13th, while a privately entered XK120 finished 11th. Commendable results now that the works teams were dominating the top 10. But even more commendable was the third place for the works Aston Martin: a genuine modified road car among the prototypes. Aston Martin, like Jaguar, did a lot for its reputation in 1951.

Less convincing but still promising was the performance of the Cunningham team. Briggs Cunningham had bought the Frick-Tappet company that had prepared his previous years' entries, moved it across country to Florida and strengthened it with a number of specialists. His was a no-expense-spared attempt to win Le Mans.

The Cunningham C1 featured a tubular frame chassis with independent front suspension using wishbones and coil springs and a de Dion rear axle. Unfortunately, Cadillac proved reluctant to supply more of its V8s so the team built four C2s with 5.4 litre Chrysler V8s (three race cars plus one spare) for the race. With 17 tons of equipment shipped in, the team was vast and its new cars were fast on the Mulsanne. However, two crashed early on. Nevertheless, at half distance the Fitch/Walters C2 lay second behind the Whitehead/Walker C-type, so the new marque had performance to back up its high profile. Sadly, bearing and valve problems dropped the car to 18th at the finish.

1951 was also a poor year for Allard – both works J2s ran off the road early on and subsequently suffered gearbox maladies. And for the splendid Bentley streamliner, which not surprisingly failed to complete the required distance to be classified. The new era belonged to Jaguar, not Bentley . . .

1.	3.4 Jaguar* (Walker/Whitehead)	6.	3.8 Healey (Rolt/Hamilton)
2.	4.5 Talbot (Meyrat/Mairesse)		* Class winners. Also:
3.	2.6 Aston Martin* (Macklin/Thompson)	12.	2.0 Lancia (Lurani/Bracco)
4.	4.5 Talbot (Levegh/Marchand)	18.	5.4 Cunningham (Walters/Fitch)
5.	2.6 Aston Martin (Abecassis/Shawe-Taylor)	21.	1.1 Porsche (Veuillet/Mouchet)
		24.	0.7 Renault (Landon/Briat)

1952

One of the greatest forces in pre-war motor racing returned in 1952 for a season of European sports car racing. Mercedes Benz bagged second place on the Mille Miglia, finished one-two-three in the Grand Prix de Berne then one-two at Le Mans. But it was no crushing performance in the French classic, more a case of profiting from the demise of others.

Ironically, Jaguar's failure was prompted by the appearance of the Mercedes 300SL on the Mille Miglia: Moss reported that the silver car had a straightline speed superiority and, mindful of the Mulsanne, Jaguar responded with a revised shape for the C-type. The car was given a longer, more steeply sloping nose and extended tail. Otherwise the Coventry challenger was little changed from its '51 specification.

The German challenger didn't prove as fast at Le Mans as had been feared but Jaguar paid the price of its late specification change. All three works cars ran too hot in practice. Although larger radiators were rigged to two of them for race day, the damage had been done. Only Ferrari had the speed to outrun the C-types and its entries didn't last. But Jaguar's reliability was even less impressive – all three entries dropped out within the first hour. After the race the revised C-type was tested with an alternative cooling system and proved 100% reliable. It had been the system devised to fit the new shape rather than the shape itself at fault.

Aston Martin likewise failed to reproduce 1951 form. Its new DB3 open cockpit 'spyder' was a disappointment. The Eberhorst car had a ladder frame chassis with torsion bar independent front suspension and de Dion rear axle and was only 50kgs lighter than the DB2 coupé. It was little quicker than the race-prepared road car and a newly enlarged, 2.9 litre engine was little tested prior to a debut race at Monaco. Three works cars were driven down to Monaco, then two survivors were driven up to Le Mans, for the 24-hour race fell only two weeks later. However, for this trip regular 2.6 engines had to be installed – the 2.9 units had failed in the Principality...

A new coupé-bodied chassis was drafted in to make up Aston Martin's Le Mans squad, to no avail. Following transmission bothers in practice the DB3 was run at a slower pace than the lightweight DB2 had averaged, yet all three examples retired with transmission failure. Macklin/Collins lasted longest, losing fourth place (which would have been third at the finish) with only three hours to run. The privately entered Clark/Keen DB2 (one of two such) was left as the marque's standard bearer and improved on its 13th place with seventh place.

It was a disappointing race for most British teams. Allard ran two new cars, clothed in all-enveloping bodies as cycle wings were no longer admissible. The modified JX2 chassis was equipped with a 260 b.h.p., 5.4 litre Chrysler 'Firepower' hemi, but neither car was fast enough and both failed, one with fuel tank bothers and a suspect bearing, the other with brake trouble.

Donald Healey lost one of his two 4.1 Nash-engined cars but saw the other, a 'spyder' (converted from the '51 coupé) entrusted to Johnson/ Wisdom run with sufficient stamina to bag the third place finish Aston Martin let slip. There was something for the British to celebrate. Not so the French or Italians.

Ferrari had a Mille Miglia winning 2.95 litre Colombo V12-engined 250S coupé for Ascari. This bored out (73 × 58.8mm) version of the original (1.5 litre) V12 produced 230 b.h.p. and the car was fast enough for the ace to set a 107.3 m.p.h. lap record. However, after two laps of glory Ascari was in the pits with clutch slip and within three hours he was out with clutch failure. The other works car was a regular 2.7 litre version of the familiar sports-racing *berlinetta* (Pagnibon/Cole) but electrical failure cost its chances. It hadn't shone, unlike Simon's NART-entered Lampredi 4.1 litre V12-engined coupé, which took a turn in the lead before it became another early pits caller. By half distance only two of seven Maranello representatives were still running. With Chinetti's 4.1 litre coupé disqualified for refuelling one lap early, and a third such car on the sidelines, only the Simon/Vincent example came through to the finish, a troubled fifth. A 340 America and a 212 were the smaller broken cars.

Ferrari had regained speed, not stamina. Talbot had an equally frustrating weekend, having to play second fiddle to a new French challenge for outright honours: Gordini. Since 1949 Amedee Gordini had chased class honours with Simca-based cars and had also raced a Simca-based 1500cc single seater in *voiturette* racing. Gradually the little four-cylinder Simca Gordinis had become more Gordini than Simca and for 1952 Gordini evolved a six-cylinder engine with d.o.h.c. which took him from 1.5 to 2.3 litres. In a light chassis this put the marque on the Le Mans pace, Manzon/Behra running the singleton entry well up in the early stages. Bigger capacity Jaguar, Ferrari and Cunningham cars having faded, the little Gordini emerged in the lead. It continued to hold sway for the best part of 12 hours before running right out of brakes...

Thankfully for France, Gordini's demise just before half distance left a Talbot in the lead. This year the three-strong works team (which had devised a smooth, all-enveloping open body shell) embraced the Levegh/Marchand partnership and, driving solo, Levegh found himself with a growing lead over the Mercedes Benz challenge when the Gordini stopped. Trying to outdo Rosier's 1950 stint of 23 hours 40 minutes, Levegh refused to hand over to Marchand, even for a brief spell. By the end of Sunday morning he had established a four lap advantage, despite frequently running out of road and scraping sand banks. With just over two hours to go the second Talbot crashed out of fifth place, but that was of little consequence. The marque was heading for another win. With just over one hour to go Levegh put his pre-selector 'box into first rather than third. The abused engine responded by breaking a con rod.

The only survivor of the four-strong Talbot representation was Chambas' familiar car, this year sporting twin Roots blowers which increased power to well over 200 b.h.p. Fast on the Mulsanne, it netted ninth.

Briggs Cunningham was another to try and outdo Rosier. He was driving one of the three new C4R designs he entered – two open cars plus a C4RK coupé. The C4R featured a significantly lighter chassis with live rear axle and a more powerful engine, but braking was a problem and over reliance on the new four-speed ZF gearbox for slowing caused the demise of the Kamm-bodied coupé in which Walters had led the first lap, before the Ferraris came through. The same problem led to the demise of one of the 'spyders' but Cunningham brought the other home – eventually assisted by Spear. He made it singlehanded through the night but when he stopped for a call of nature the following morning Spear pinched a drive!

The surviving Cunningham took fourth, behind the Nash Healey and those sturdy Mercedes 300SLs.

Daimler Benz had been left shattered by the war but by 1952 had made great strides and had introduced a 2.2 litre six-cylinder sports coupé to complement its range of luxury saloon cars. This was a short chassis derivative of its 300 saloon and thus featured independent front suspension by coil springs and swinging half shafts at the rear. Research and development chief Rudolf Uhlenhaut was given the task of proving it in competition in 1952 and took the Jaguar route of developing a special chassis around which to hang its mechanicals. The 300SL *(Sport Leicht)* featured a sophisticated small diameter tube spaceframe clad with a coupé body that had unusual gullwing doors. Its 300S engine was tuned to produce 175 b.h.p. and was inclined in the chassis to keep the bonnet line low.

Although it had finished second on the Mille Miglia and won Berne, the 300SL's Swiss victory had been after the retirement of its only serious opponent, a works Ferrari. At Le Mans an unmodified C-type would almost certainly have beaten the 'silver arrows'. As it was, under the guidance of legendary Team Manager Neubauer, Mercedes ran conservatively and consistently to victory. The team lost one car (Kling/Klenk) but Lang/Riess came home ahead of Helfrich/Niedermayer to score a memorable triumph. Jaguar could but wait for the following year...

1.	3.0 Mercedes-Benz* (Lang/Riess)	6.	2.0 Lancia* (Valenzano/Ippocambo)
2.	3.0 Mercedes-Benz (Helfrich/Niedermayer)	* Class winners. Also:	
		11.	1.1 Porsche
3.	4.1 Nash-Healey* (Johnson/Wisdom)		(Veuillet/Mouche)
		13.	1.5 Jowett
4.	5.4 Cunningham* (Cunningham/Spear)		(Becquart/Wilkins)
		14.	0.6 Panhard
5.	4.1 Ferrari (Simon/Vincent)		(Hemard/Dussous)

1953

It has been called the triumph of the disc brake. More accurately, it was the triumph of Jaguar's endurance racing philosophy. A good, solid car based on well proven components. That was the winning formula.

Ironically, the C-type's chances hadn't been highly rated. After the previous year's debacle the team cars had been run in the Goodwood Nine Hours to try to regain some lost pride on home soil, but all three had again failed and 1953 had commenced with a fruitless sortie to Italy's gruelling Mille Miglia...

Nevertheless, Jaguar knew that the C-type was inherently a sound design, whereas the rival V12 Ferrari had to be considered fast but somewhat fragile. For '53 the C-type had been lightened somewhat and had reverted to a more conservative body design – the '52 shape had been more slippery but had caused high speed instability. The engine had its twin SU carburettors replaced by triple twin-choke Webers which yielded an extra 10 b.h.p. and considerably more torque, and Dunlop's new disc brake replaced the traditional drum.

Leading the newly instigated World Sports Car Championship, of which Le Mans was round three, thanks to victory by a 4.1 litre coupé on the Mille Miglia, Ferrari replied with a brand new car, the 375MM. This had 100mm longer frame and a 4.5 litre (84mm bore) version of the Lampredi V12 which the designer had developed for the previous year's Indianapolis 500. Still breathing through three Webers, its 320 b.h.p. (78 b.h.p. per litre) propelled the regular layout, unsophisticated Maranello sports-racing chassis, with Pinin Farina enclosed bodywork, down the Mulsanne at only a shade under 150 m.p.h. But, in spite of a 100 b.h.p. deficit, the more efficiently shaped C-type was only 1 m.p.h. slower, according to the ACO's speed check. Around the rest of the course superior cornering and braking offset the C-type's inferior acceleration.

After only four laps, Moss' C-type forced past Villoresi's sole 375MM. Moss/Walker hit fuel feed problems within the first hour but once Rolt spotted their car in the pits he put his example ahead of the Italian car. Thereafter the race featured a tremendous duel between Rolt/Hamilton and Villoresi/Ascari which went right through the night.

The 375MM set fastest lap but the Jaguar had the upper hand (thanks partly to more secure braking) and by breakfast time on Sunday it had a two lap margin. Both cars made routine stops around 8.30 a.m. As the Ferrari set off again it was heard to have a slipping clutch. Within two hours it was out.

Three key figures in the rise of the Jaguar Le Mans campaign (from left to right) Walker (cup in hand), Moss and 'Lofty' England. Photo: LAT.

The Villoresi/Ascari 375MM had been the longest-lived of the two Ferrari favourites – the Hawthorn/Farina (4.1 litre) 340MM had been disqualified for replenishing too soon, after further raising the lap record. A third works car, another 4.1 litre (all three with lengthened chassis) in the hands of the Marzotto brothers, was driving a steady race. Tragically, Cole had been killed when his 340MM, the only private Ferrari in the race, had overturned in mist at White House around 6.30 a.m.

The Villoresi/Ascari retirement promoted Moss/Walker to second place, this duo having dropped to 21st position in the early stages through two stops to clear fuel lines. With no further worries, the Jaguars came home first, second and fourth, the Rolt/Hamilton car the first ever to win at over 100 m.p.h., with an average of 105.85 m.p.h. Ferrari's only consolation was fifth place for the Marzotto brothers.

Splitting the Jaguar formation was the best-placed Cunningham, the new CR5 of Walters/Fitch. Dubbed 'The Shark', it featured slab sided bodywork and a revised, Indy Car-influenced front end, utilising what was, in effect, a de Dion arrangement. Like its sister cars, a C4R crewed

In winning the 1953 race, the C-type Jaguar of Rolt and Hamilton became the first car to average over 100mph. Photo: Jaguar.

by Cunningham/Spear and the coupé-bodied C4RK in the hands of Morgan/Bennett, it was equipped with massive drum brakes. Although the Shark was fractionally faster than the C-type of the Mulsanne, none of the American runners could match the pace of the leading British and Italian cars but all came home, the C4R in seventh place, the C4RK 10th.

The Cunninghams had been outrun by the impressive spaceframe 'Disco Volante' (flying saucer) Alfa Romeo, which was the fastest car on the Mulsanne at 150.88 m.p.h. One example proved capable of keeping the leading duo in sight on Saturday evening. However, driven by Kling/Riess, it went out before half distance due to clutch failure, while the equally rapid Fangio/Marimon example had expired within two hours of the start. With Sanesi/Carini also out before half distance, the quick 3.5 litre car had a fruitless Le Mans debut.

Equally disappointing was the performance of the new D20 Lancia. Gianni Lancia's works team had won 2.0 litre honours in '51 and '52 with its Aurelia coupés so held high hopes for its first proper sports-racer, a V6-engined *Competitizione Berlinetta* designed by innovative ex-Alfa

Ferrari's 1953 challenger, the 375MM, had massive 4.5 litre V12 engine good for over 300bhp, but the poor aerodynamics of its Pininfarina coupé body left it unable to shake off the C-type, 100bhp weaker but only 1mph slower on the Mulsanne. Photo: LAT.

Romeo engineer Jano. Alas, all four 2.7 litre supercharged entries fell by the wayside without having made a real mark.

If the race was disappointing for the proud Italian factories, it was equally sad for the French hopes. Neither Talbot nor Gordini was a serious threat, but Gordini did salvage a worthy sixth place for its 2.5 litre runner. The best that Levegh could manage this year was a steady eighth place, sharing with Pozzi: a new regulation demanded that a driver do no more than 80 laps consecutively and no more than 18 hours in total. The three other Talbot entries broke. With slightly more power, Chambas' old warrior spun on lap 24 and had to be driven two miles in reverse, which proved too much for its gearbox. That was a sad end to a long Le Mans career.

Behind the Levegh/Pozzi Talbot was the highest of the second-string British runners, a production C-type (essentially to '51 specification) run by Jacques Swaters' Belgian-based Ecurie Francorchamps. The only other big-engined British cars to finish were one of two Nash Healeys, in 11th position, and a pair of near standard 2.6 litre Austin Healeys, which took 3.0 litre class runner-up honours with 12th and 14th places, well behind the class-winning Gordini racers.

Allard ran two works JRs but the new Cadillac-powered devices failed. Allard had actually held the lead at the end of lap one but failed to make the end of lap two – the hurriedly prepared car's rear axle mounting broke. The other car overheated, then retired at quarter distance through con rod failure.

All three Aston Martins also retired. The marque held high hopes following its first major international win in the '52 Goodwood Nine Hours and for '53 a smaller, lighter DB3S was developed by Willie Watson to accept the revised 2.9 litre six, which now gave a dependable 180 b.h.p. Alas, due to lack of development time the new chassis was not on the Le Mans pace and Parnell crashed his example after only 16 laps. Abecassis/Salvadori retired with clutch slip after an unmemorable run, while Poore/Thompson lasted longest – 182 laps – after which they lay only 14th due to long stops to replace broken tappets. A walking wounded, this car expired due to an overheating engine.

For Aston Martin things could only get better, while for Jaguar similarly there was only one way to go ... To ensure it didn't go *that* way, the triumphant marque was planning something very special for 1954 ...

1.	3.4 Jaguar* (Rolt/Hamilton)	6.	2.5 Gordini* (Trintignant/Schell)
2.	3.4 Jaguar (Moss/Walker)		* Class winners. Also:
3.	5.5 Cunningham* (Fitch/Walters)	13.	2.0 Frazer-Nash (Wharton/Mitchell)
4.	3.4 Jaguar (Whitehead/Stewart)	15.	1.5 Porsche (von Frankenberg/Frere)
5.	4.1 Ferrari (Marzotto/Marzotto)	17.	0.7 DB (Bonnet/Moynet)
		18.	1.1 Osca (Damonte/Helde)

1954

Britain versus Italy: Jaguar versus Ferrari once again. Aston Martin still could not produce the goods and although Italy had Alfa Romeo, Lancia and Maserati active in international competition (the latter fielding 2.0 litre cars) it was once more left to Ferrari to defend its Le Mans honour. Nevertheless, the battle for supremacy was once again a Homeric one, both contenders fielding powerful new weapons.

Ferrari unloaded three big 375 Plus cars, featuring a new frame design, a de Dion rear end (suspended by a transverse leaf spring) and a curvaceous spyder body by Pinin Farina. But more significant was the Lampredi V12 – with bigger bore it now displaced 4954cc and power was approaching 350 b.h.p. That was transmitted via a four-speed gearbox in unit with the final drive and the entire package weighed 1000kgs. The 375 Plus had been produced to win Le Mans *and* the Mille Miglia but the Italian classic had turned into a debacle – Lancia's 240 b.h.p. challenger boasted a similar power:weight ratio and better road holding – and neither 375 Plus had made the finish . . .

Jaguar replied at Le Mans with three of its brand new model, the D-type. This had a striking, functional aerodynamic shape devised by company stylist Malcolm Sayer. It was extremely slippery yet proved stable and by careful design (including canting the engine over, Mercedes style, by eight degrees) the frontal area had been kept well below that of the C-type. The D-type was also sophisticated in chassis construction. The skin around the open cockpit was stressed, the middle portion of the car being of monocoque construction. The engine and front suspension were hung on the front of a tubular frame which extended through the aircraft style monocoque, acting as a backbone. The frame terminated at the back in a bulkhead which carried the rear suspension. The suspension design was reminiscent of that employed on the C-type and the live rear axle looked positively dated. Nevertheless, Le Mans was fast and smooth and strength and dependability were considered more important than agile handling.

Under the low bonnet line was the familiar 3442cc six, unfashionably under square at 83mm × 106mm. It was now dry sumped, which helped it keep a low profile, and had been coaxed to produce 250 b.h.p., which was fed through a new, all-synchromesh gearbox. Naturally, Dunlop discs provided retardation.

The D-type was finished too late for serious testing prior to the marathon but Jaguar was able to snatch a few laps of private testing at the circuit and went five seconds under Ascari's record. The improved shape and extra power saw Moss' example fastest on the Mulsanne, come race weekend. Speeds had jumped above 170 m.p.h. – the British lad was timed at 172.97. Nevertheless, the extra power of the Ferrari kept the Italian car well in touch, and its sheer acceleration gave it an edge in the dry. Thankfully, for Jaguar, a good portion of the race was wet. Then the D-type's superior controllability was decisive.

Gonzales left no time in showing the superiority of the potent 375 Plus in the dry, when its hydraulically assisted drums were an answer to Jaguar's discs. At three hours the 375 Plus trio lay first, second and third. However, it then started to rain. Moss took command for Jaguar, passing the red cars as the track gradually became wetter. But again came early trouble for Jaguar – its three cars were delayed by a fuel feed problem, traced to over-efficient filters. Then Moss ran out of brakes at the end of the Mulsanne and eventually Wharton/Whitehead lost most of their gears, both misfortunes leading to retirement. So once again it came down to Rolt/Hamilton versus Ferrari's best.

The Maglioli/Marzotto 375 Plus retired at 11 p.m. with a broken gearbox and the Rosier/Manzon example was destined to go that way too – it was eventually withdrawn at dawn, stuck in second. However, Gonzales/Trintignant held sway overnight and Rolt/Hamilton soldiered on in pursuit, taking up where their teammates had left off. At half distance, helped by wet weather, the Jaguar was in striking distance and before long had the 375 Plus right in its sights. However, an incident with a slower car at 10.30 a.m. sent the D-type into its pit and suggested that perhaps the Gods really were on Ferrari's side, after all.

Rolt/Hamilton had worked their way onto the lead lap before the incident, which cost over a lap; by the time the ACO clock showed 2.00 p.m. the Ferrari was looking unassailable, two laps ahead on a dry track. Then it started to rain again. The Ferrari started to lose compression and after the last round of pit stops refused to fire up!

Gonzales climbed back onto the pit counter, the mechanics opened the bonnet for the first time in the race and worked anxiously, then sealed it again and the driver made another attempt to rejoin the fray . . . The Ferrari remained lifeless. Meanwhile, Rolt was pulling in for fresh goggles only for the Jaguar crew frantically to wave him on.

The D-type unlapped itself and, with wet electrics further soaked, the 375 stubbornly continued to refuse to fire up. However, just before the British car was due to come into sight once more, this time to regain the lead, the V12 relented, bellowing into life. Gonzales slingshot away and Rolt, unable to see properly, stopped, to be replaced by Hamilton.

Some magnificent, adrenalin-soaked wet weather driving kept the Ferrari in front and, with the track drying over the last half-an-hour, the Gods really had come down on Maranello's side. Nevertheless, Hamilton brought the pride of Coventry home less than two minutes in arrears.

It was suggested that the Jaguar team might protest at the number of mechanics working on the 375 Plus during its agonizing final stop – a wide body of opinion had it that Ferrari had over-stepped the mandatory mark. There was also a suggestion that the team had worked on the car while the engine had been running. However, Sir William Lyons dismissed any idea of protest, not wishing to beat his opponents in the court room.

Ferrari had avenged its 1953 defeat, even if it had lost four of its five runners. The failed customer cars were a 375MM with big bore, 340 American engine (Baggio/Rubirosa), which was extracted from a sandbank early in the race only to lapse onto 11 cylinders, and a modified 340 America run by Briggs Cunningham which retired through rear axle failure on Sunday morning.

Cunningham had planned to run a Ferrari-engined Cunningham but the project had fallen behind schedule. Instead, it had two C4Rs featuring modified bodywork and water-cooled drums: Dunlop wouldn't supply it discs. Once again the team looked to reliability, profiting from the misfortunes of others to collect a worthy third place (Spear/Johnson) and fifth place (Cunningham/Bennett).

Splitting the American cars was the Ecurie Francorchamps entered private C-type, the Belgian team overshadowing the home runners. Gordini lost its disc-braked 3.0 litre, eight cylinder runner, but again bagged sixth with its class-winning 2.5 litre six. Talbot was less competitive, only one of three private entries making it past half distance. The quickest, in Levegh's hands, had been an early retirement.

While Talbot was falling from grace through lack of development work, Aston Martin had no such reason for a lacklustre performance. Unlike the ailing Talbot marque, it still had the luxury of a vigorous competition programme and could amass no less than six representatives at La Sarthe. Highest hope was for a pair of DB3 S models with new coupé bodies and improved 190 b.h.p. engines. After the disappointing '53 race the DB3S had finished the season winning every race in which it had taken part. The improved cars for '54 featured outboard brakes and alongside them the factory ran a pair of open-bodied '53 models (one standard and in the hands of new owner Shelby, the other supercharged in a desperate search for speed that was anticipated to be at the cost of longevity) *plus* a '53-type car with a new 4.5 litre 'Lagonda' V12 engine. At the same time it was supporting a privately run DB2/4 coupé.

The Lagonda car fell victim to accident damage early on and the new coupé chassis, although more slippery, was less stable than the standard car, possibly explaining the retirement of both examples through crashes at White House. The Shelby car fell out with a broken stub axle, leaving but one car in pursuit of Cunningham at dawn – the supercharged model. To the team's surprise, it lasted almost until midday...

Now without Eberan, Aston Martin was still in the doldrums. While Jaguar and Ferrari were on the crest of a wave.

1.	5.0 Ferrari* (Gonzales/Trintignant)	6.	2.5 Gordini* (Guelfi/Pollet)
2.	3.4 Jaguar (Rolt/Hamilton)		* Class winners. Also:
3.	5.5 Cunningham* (Spear/Johnston)	7.	2.0 Bristol (Mayers/Wilson)
4.	3.4 Jaguar (Swaters/Laurent)	10.	0.7 DB-Panhard (Bonnet/Bayol)
5.	5.5 Cunningham (Benett/Cunningham)	12.	1.5 Porsche (Claes/Strasse)
		14.	1.1 Porsche (Duntov/Olivier)

1955

Mercedes Benz had a knack of winning. Its advanced W196 Grand Prix car hadn't been the fastest of '54 but had amassed four wins from seven races. The marque had gone on to win the first three '55 races and to give a spin-off sports car, the W196-S, a winning debut on the Mille Miglia.

The W196-S was more commonly known as the 300SLR but *wasn't* a development of the old 300SL. It was a very close relative of the Grand Prix car with a 3.0 litre version of the sophisticated 2.5 litre fuel-injected, desmodromic valve, split crank straight eight, which produced an honest 100 b.h.p./litre. It had widened W196 spaceframe chassis with all-round independent suspension, using torsion bars and inboard mounted drum brakes. The engine was canted for a low bonnet line (as with Jaguar but more steeply).

In practice the sophisticated silver German car was tried with a novel extra: a tonneau cover which flipped up at the driver's command to provide an air brake! With 300 b.h.p. and 168 m.p.h. on the Mulsanne, the new German car was a very keen competitor for the D-type and the latest six-cylinder Ferrari.

Six cylinders? Why not... The in-line six configuration had worked well for Jaguar and Ferrari's 2.5 litre four-cylinder Grand Prix engine had produced good performance in '54: Lampredi had taken that engine and added two extra pots. That move took capacity to 3750cc and, breathing through three Webers, the d.o.h.c. Ferrari six produced 280 b.h.p. (75 b.h.p. per litre).

That wasn't enough to out-perform the 375 Plus. The Mille Miglia had seen the debut of a bigger displacement version: 4412cc produced an honest 360 b.h.p. (81 per litre).

The new straight six engines propelled a significantly smaller, lighter chassis design than that of the superceded V12 car. For example, whereas the 375 Plus had sat on a 2600mm wheelbase, the new sixes (Tipo 118LM (3750cc) and 121LM) squatted within a 2400mm measurement. With five-speed gearbox feeding a de Dion rear end and sleeker, D-type influenced lines, the bigger displacement version had been the fastest car in its debut race. Three sixes were readied for Le Mans and Castellotti's 121 was clocked at over 175 m.p.h. in practice.

In reply, Jaguar offered a slightly refined D-type, with longer nose, mildly modified overall shape and big valve heads worth 270 b.h.p. (79 per litre). The new profile allowed it to reach 175 m.p.h. – but with an extra litre, the Ferrari was a fraction faster. The Italian car also boasted

Mercedes came, saw... but withdrew mid-race following the involvement of Levegh's 300SLR in the tragic accident of 1955. This is the sister car of Kling/Simon. Photo: LAT.

superior acceleration. However, the Jaguar had staying power that the other six had yet to demonstrate. By half distance the Maranello challenge had failed.

Thanks to proven reliability, Coventry had Maranello beating capability. But did it have Stuttgart beating capability, too? The question remains unanswered.

When, at 6.30 p.m., Levegh's 300SLR collided with Macklin's little Austin Healey (which was changing direction to avoid Hawthorn's pit-bound D-type), the lead was in dispute between Hawthorn and Fangio's 300SLR, this pair having gradually drawn away from the fastest 121, that of Castelloti, which had led the opening laps.

When, at 2.00 a.m., Mercedes Team Manager Neubauer withdrew his two remaining cars as a mark of respect to the 80 or more killed in the horrifying Levegh/Macklin accident, the Fangio/Moss car held a two-lap lead over Hawthorn/Bueb, who went on to win. Ferrari had lost not only its three works 121s, but also two private 750 Monzas (one of them run by Cunningham), the five-strong Italian force hit by drivetrain and cylinder head failures.

Jaguar went on to lose two of three works cars. Dewis/Beauman fell foul of accident damage, while Rolt/Hamilton inherited second spot with the Mercedes withdrawal, only to suffer a split oil tank, then a seized gearbox. A Cunningham-run D-type and a Jaguar-powered Cooper also fell by the wayside but, having switched from C- to D-type, Francor-champs went one better than in '54 to finish third.

Second place was a surprise: an Aston Martin DB3 S. The marque had reverted to open bodies (saving weight), had fitted discs and had found a genuine 210 b.h.p. from its 2.9 litre six. Not enough to run with the leaders, but enough to get a reliable car home in a strong position.

Aston Martin also ran its V12 engine in a new spaceframe open car but 'Project 166' was only marginally faster and the unique car ran out of fuel.

Two of the three DB3 S fell out before half distance. At that point the survivor (Collins/Frere) was battling with a Maserati in the wake of the one healthy D-type. Maserati had entered a single 2.0 litre car for the previous year's race, but that had retired on Sunday morning. Its new, multi-tubular spaceframe 300S had a 3.0 litre in-line six, this longer stroke version of its 250F Grand Prix car's unit producing a claimed 250 b.h.p. Two of the de Dion rear axle cars (with Giulio Alfieri chassis based closely on the 250F) had been entered, backed by a 2.0 litre 'A6GCS'. At half distance it was the Musso/Valenzano 3.0 litre car still running, holding Aston Martin off for second, if 20 m.p.h. down on Jaguar's Mulsanne speed. The battle for second was a close affair until clutch failure cost the Italian car's chances – after it had got within three laps of Hawthorn/Bueb following an off-road excursion by the Jaguar on Sunday morning.

The Aston Martin came home 40 miles behind the works Jaguar but 50 miles ahead of the private D-type, to record the marque's first finish since 1951. Perseverance pays.

Perhaps Cunningham wasn't so patient... his fast Walters/Spear pairing had been occupied in the unsuccessful production D-type (engine failure). His team had run but one example of its new C6, in which an Offenhauser 3.0 litre engine replaced the planned Ferrari V12 following a disagreement somewhere between the USA and Italy. The 'Offy' was a methanol Indy engine converted to run on petrol – and the C6R had turned out to be slower than the C4R...

The 1955 race was one of attrition among the leading runners which, combined with Mercedes' withdrawal, left the pickings behind the top three finishers to be collected by small-engined cars. Most successful was a trio of 1.5 litre Porsches which filled out the top six: a splendid result for the growing Zuffenhausen marque which had made its first Le Mans entry in 1951.

1955 was a race without a Talbot or Gordini challenge for outright honours – and only a sole 2.0 litre Gordini to represent France. It was a race that left the nation and the world shocked. Could there be another Le Mans?

1.	3.4 Jaguar*	6.	1.5 Porsche
	(Hawthorn/Bueb)		(Juhan/Glockler)
2.	2.9 Aston Martin*		* Class winners. Also:
	(Collins/Frere)	7.	2.0 Bristol
3.	3.4 Jaguar		(Mayers/Wilson)
	(Swaters/Claes)	13.	1.1 Porsche
4.	1.5 Porsche*		(Duntov/Veuillet)
	(von Frankenberg/Polensky)	16.	0.7 DB-Panhard
5.	1.5 Porsche		(Cornet/Mougin)
	(Seidel/Gendebien)		

1956

The tragic 1955 race led to a ban on motor racing in France, but this was lifted following an enquiry into the disaster and it was left to the ACO to take appropriate action to improve the safety of its 24-hour race. The club reconstructed the inadequate pits area and imposed stringent new regulations aimed at slowing the cars. The cars were hit with a fuel ration and a capacity limit of 2.5 litres on prototypes. The fuel measure took the form of a maximum tank size of 130 litres and a minimum run of 34 laps between stops, calling for an m.p.g. of 10.83. In addition, international sports car regulations had been modified slightly and the cars now had to sport a full width windscreen.

Le Mans was alone in its 2.5 litre capacity limit and, coupled with the withdrawal of Mercedes Benz and Lancia from the sport and the demise of the Cunningham marque, the net result was a drastic reduction in the number of potential winners.

Jaguar claimed to have constructed more than 50 D-types and Aston Martin made a similar assertion about its DB3 S output, so these prototypes were classified as production sports cars, thereby skirting around the capacity limit. Not so fortunate were Ferrari (which had taken over the resources of the Lancia competition department), Gordini and Maserati, and Maserati was content to supply 2.5 litre engines to Talbot, still struggling to maintain a Le Mans presence.

Practice revealed that the 3.4 litre D-type was at least four seconds a lap faster than the 3.0 litre DB3 S, which in turn could comfortably outrun the smaller capacity 'prototype' opposition. With five D-types heading the line-up, the race looked a foregone conclusion. However, it started on a treacherously damp surface and on the second lap Frere spun his works D-type into the bank at the Esses. Teammate Fairman took avoiding action, only to be hit by a works Ferrari driven by the Marquis de Portago. All three cars were *hors de combat*.

Soon afterwards, the last surviving works D-type began a series of pit stops, trying to cure a misfire. It was eventually traced to a hairline crack in a fuel line but by then the car had lost 21 laps. The setbacks for the works Jaguar team left Aston Martin's fastest pairing of Moss/Collins in front, chased hard by the Ecurie Ecosse D-type of Flockhart/Sanderson. The private Jaguar didn't have the big valve engine but did have the latest works chassis modifications, which included a rear anti-roll bar and carefully shaped full width screen to minimise the drag caused by the mandatory new fitment. The Aston Martin it was chasing was at the end of its development and was in service as a stop-gap measure, while a new DBR1 prototype underwent preparation. However, the DB3 S 'homologation' was useful at Le Mans and, remember, both Aston Martin and Jaguar had to sacrifice speed to fuel economy in this race...

Before dark the 3.4 litre car went ahead and it took the considerable talents of Moss and Collins to keep the Aston Martin in touch overnight. The English professionals lost second gear on Sunday morning and could then but pray for rain...

A dry track allowed the Scottish amateurs to gallop home to victory by a slender but significant one-lap margin. The second works DB3 S of Salvadori/Walker crashed upside down, as did the 'Project 166' development car, which was running to the 2.5 litre prototype limit. Third place was taken by the sole survivor of a three-car Ferrari prototype team, which beat the second private D-type, that of Ecurie Francorchamps.

Ferrari had concocted three special spyder-bodied prototypes for the occasion using as a basis its 'Touring' 2.0 litre chassis plus its '625' 2.5 litre Grand Prix engine. The Formula One in-line four had been shunned for the Grand Prix programme in favour of the newly inherited Lancia V8 and was good for no more than 225 b.h.p. (90 per litre). Lampredi had left and successors Bellentani and Fraschetti had produced a 3.5 litre version of his Formula One four and a new 3.5 litre V12 for international sports car racing, but neither could be taken to La Sarthe. Worse, Ferrari's stand-in sports-racing chassis was equipped with a full width windscreen of poor aerodynamic properties, adding up to a Mulsanne speed of less than 145 m.p.h., whereas the D-type could still exceed 155 m.p.h.

Start of the 1956 race with the Moss Aston Martin quick enough off the No. 8 mark to challenge pole sitter Hawthorn's D type. Flockhart's similar Jaguar (car No. 4) gives hot pursuit. Photo: LAT.

The second lap retirement of de Portago's '625LM' had been followed by a broken transmission on the Simon/Hill sister car, leaving the Gendebien/Trintignant example to collect Ferrari's third place consolation. The traditional French marques, Gordini and Talbot, had no such consolation Gordini even though it had considerable experience of a 2.5 litre prototype. Neither its six- nor its eight-cylinder runner made it through the night. Talbot used a Maserati six, which the Italian company was happy to supply as it was busy developing a 4.5 litre car for the World Championship, of which Le Mans was not a part this year. Talbot competitions manager Zehender shared one Talbot-Maserati with Lucas, who crashed the car early in the race, while the other example in the hands of Behra/Rosier broke its rear axle soon after midnight.

The way was left open behind the top four finishers for another strong showing by a 1.5 litre Porsche. This outperformed five cars of 2.0/2.3 litres capacity – including three second-string Ferrari entries – to bag fifth. Hot on its heels was the recovering works D-type in which Hawthorn set fastest lap. Alas, the early set-back had been too great for the car to end its works career on a high note. The factory had decided that in future teams like Ecurie Ecosse would defend the marque's Le Mans honour. And although Ecurie Ecosse had proved itself equal to the challenge, it could expect a tough time ahead, for the race was to revert to World Championship status, once more admitting unlimited capacity prototypes...

1.	3.4 Jaguar*	5.	1.5 Porsche*
	(Flockhart/Sanderson)		(Von Trips/von Frankenberg)
2.	3.0 Aston Martin*	6.	3.4 Jaguar
	(Moss/Collins)		(Hawthorn/Bueb)
3.	2.5 Ferrari	* Class winners. Also:	
	(Gendebien/Trintignant)	7.	1.1 Lotus-Climax
4.	3.4 Jaguar		(Jopp/Bicknell)
	(Swaters/Rousselle)	10.	DB-Panhard
			(Laureau/Armagnac)

1957

Return to the World Championship arena brought Le Mans the struggle between Titans developed by Ferrari and Maserati. Jaguar hadn't the power to compete with the bigger displacement Italian cars, nor had Aston Martin's new DBR1. 1957 was about 4.0 litre V12 (335) Ferrari versus 4.5 litre V8 (450) Maserati and the opening laps of the 24-hour marathon were run at record speed. For the first time in its history, the circuit was lapped in less than four minutes.

The works Ferraris of Collins (Hill) and Hawthorn (Musso) were the early leaders. Their V12 engines were d.o.h.c. units developed from the 3.5 litre engine that ex-Lancia engineer Jano had helped develop in '56. Less highly stressed than the alternative 3.5 litre four, the new V12 had been Ferrari's winning edge in the 1956 World Championship. 1957 had brought a 3.8 litre then a full 4023cc version, which repeated the 3.5 litre's Mille Miglia success. The most significant aspect of the 4.0 litre version was not its sheer size but the fact that it was the first Ferrari four cam for sports car racing. Breathing through six Webers it produced 390 b.h.p. (97 per litre). However, there was a question mark over its dependability. And Collins' example only lasted three laps...

Hawthorn led until a wheelbearing had to be changed on lap 20. Then his engine seized...

The demise of the fast Ferraris left the field clear for the Maserati *Tipo* 54, more commonly known as the 450S. Developed by Alfieri to replace the underpowered 300S, its 4478cc d.o.h.c., 90 degree V8 was reckoned to produce as much as 420 b.h.p. (94 per litre), breathing through four Webers. Its chassis was a beefed-up 300S with new de Dion rear end and five-speed transaxle but, like Ferrari, Maserati still relied upon drum braking.

And, like Ferrari, Maserati lacked staying power. Moss/Schell's example, sporting Frank Costin-designed coupé bodywork, was soon delayed by a split oil line and rejoined only to be added to the list of early retirements through c.v. failure. A similar breakage claimed the leading open version in the hands of Behra/Simon...

1957 might have been the year of the Big Bangers but by nightfall Le Mans was in familiar hands. The Jaguar D-type was short on power with no more than 300 b.h.p. from its familiar straight six but it was fast on the Mulsanne in new 3.8 litre guise (matching the 170 m.p.h.-plus speeds reached by the less aerodynamically efficient Italian cars) and in both 3.4 and 3.8 litre trim was a reliable proposition. Five examples were running, two with the new 3780cc block, the main advantages of which were more torque and an extra 10 m.p.h. on the Mulsanne...

The 3.8 cars were entered by Ecurie Ecosse (Flockhart/Bueb) and Duncan Hamilton (owner/Gregory). The latter lost time early on to an exhaust problem but the Scottish-entered car was in a position to inherit the lead with the failure of the last Italian car. Second-string Ferraris, Maserati's back-up 300S and a quartet of Aston Martins were its most serious threats.

Ferrari had backed up its 335s with a 3.8 litre '315' and a '250 Testa Rossa', the latter a prototype for the car Ferrari planned to run under a forthcoming 3.0 litre World Sports Car Championship capacity limit. It used a development of the Colombo V12 and its open body was of 'sponson' style with wings cut away behind the front wheels for under bonnet cooling and long nose jutting ahead of the wings.

The 250 Testa Rossa moved up to second overall, behind the Scottish Jaguar, only quickly to fall victim to yet more Maranello piston trouble. The only dependable member of the Ferrari fleet (which included a 3.5 litre car run by the Equipe Nationale Belge) was the Lewis Evans/Severi 315, which was hampered by brake problems and was no match for the D-type. It finished fifth.

Maserati's 3.0 litre six didn't feature and its clutch exploded to complete a knock-out for the works team, a feat that was matched by Aston Martin.

The British factory likewise ran three cars – two 250 b.h.p., 2.9 litre DBR1s plus a DBR2. The latter was a last-minute effort to find more speed: it married the 'Project 166' spaceframe chassis with a 3.7 litre d.o.h.c. six designed by Tadek Merek for a forthcoming road car. Entrusted to the brothers Whitehead, its new engine was afflicted by fuel starvation problems which didn't allow it to show its 290 b.h.p. potential. It failed, as anticipated.

More noteworthy was the DBR1. This had a Ted Cutting-designed spaceframe chassis (replacing the ladder frame of the DB3 S) and refined DB3 S suspension. It had a transaxle combining gearbox and final drive (from Project 166) and new 'spyder' body shape. With heavily revised 3.0 litre six now producing 270 b.h.p. the DBR1 had made a winning debut at Spa the previous month, and had backed that up with victory in the Nurburgring 1000kms, this time against Ferrari and Maserati opposition, sheer power not being a decisive factor on the German mountain course. Alas, the model had yet to develop 24-hour staying power and both examples got stuck in fourth gear. The faster version, in the hands of Brooks/Cunningham-Reid, ran second to the Ecurie Ecosse D-type through the hours of darkness until 2.00 a.m., when its transmission bug struck, pitching it off the road at Terte Rouge...

In the second half of the race the well proven D-types had a near monopoly of the leader board, the result a certainty for Coventry. A poor entry from France of one 3.0 litre Gordini and one 2.5 litre Talbot-Maserati had proved no threat – the Italian-engined car had even suffered the humiliation of breaking its clutch on the line!

In the wake of the Ecurie Ecosse 3.8 litre D-type, an ENB 3.4 car crewed by Frere/Rousselle demoted the Scottish team's second entry

(Lawrence/Sanderson) overnight, only to lose an hour around three-quarters distance due to broken points. Rousselle had lost power out at Mulsanne corner and it had taken a long while to diagnose the fault: the car dropped to fifth, but overhauled the failing Ferrari 315 to complete a clean sweep of the top four positions for Jaguar.

In third place, behind the victorious Ecurie Ecosse cars, was the French-entered example of Jean-Marie Brussin (Brussin/Lucas). The delayed Hamilton car recovered to claim sixth. Still, five out of five was quite a finishing record . . .

Overseen by familiar factory personnel, headed by Lofty England, the rugged D-type had enjoyed its most successful year ever, and a fifth victory for Jaguar matched Bentley's claim. With a 3.0 litre capacity limit looming, could the old warrior roll to further honours?

1.	3.8 Jaguar*		* Class winner. Also:
	(Flockhart/Bueb)	7.	2.0 Ferrari
2.	3.4 Jaguar		(Bianchi/Harris)
	(Sanderson/Lawrence)	8.	1.5 Porsche
3.	3.4 Jaguar		(Hugus/Beaufort)
	(Mary/Lucas)	9.	1.1 Lotus-Climax
4.	3.4 Jaguar		(Chamberlain/Mackay-Fraser)
	(Frere/Rousselle)	11.	2.9 Aston Martin
5.	3.8 Ferrari		(Colas/Kerguen)
	(Severi/Lewis-Evans)	14.	0.7 Lotus-Climax
6.	3.4 Jaguar		(Allison/Hall)
	(Hamilton/Gregory)		

1958

Aston Martin lost its best chance to date. The 3.0 litre capacity limit put its DBR1 right in the ball park. The now well developed car was more than a match for the Ferrari 250 Testa Rossa: the British marque rubbed that home with an easy victory in the Nurburgring 1000kms early in its short '58 campaign. Having won the German classic as he pleased, Moss proceeded to lead the Testa Rossas at Le Mans – all ten of them – without undue effort. Alas, after two hours his straight six cried enough. A broken con rod handed the race to the Italian horde.

Worse, in some respects, for the British factory, a privately entered DB3 S driven by the Whiteheads outlasted all three team cars and, thanks to a high rate of attrition, found itself second at the finish. If only the Salvadori/Lewis Evans DBR1 hadn't slid off the road or the Brooks/Trintignant DBR1 hadn't suffered transmission failure, this could so easily have been Aston Martin's year. Second place was no consolation in such circumstances...

So it was down to Ferrari, challenged only by a private Jaguar. Having narrowly lost the 1957 world title, Maserati had retired through commercial pressure and the Talbot and Gordini days were over. Enthusiasts like Antonio Lago and Amedee Gordini were having to sell out to large concerns to survive in a changing automotive environment.

Mind you, given its high rate of failure, Ferrari had to count itself lucky to have won, particularly as overnight rain helped Duncan Hamilton's D-type to get into contention. There again, one strong finish out of ten cars isn't so hard to achieve...

Three of the ten were works cars. After the demise of the Moss/Brabham DBR1 they lay one-two-three: Collins/Hawthorn – Gendebien/Hill – von Trips/Seidel. The 250 Testa Rossa was a proven package and in the absence of Aston Martin had won the early season races, Buenos Aires and the Targa Florio. It had also won the Sebring 12-hours following the failure of the DBR1.

While the customer cars still carried a live axle at the back of the traditional ladder frame, the works now had a de Dion rear end. All examples had independent front suspension with coil springs and around 300 b.h.p. (100 per litre) from the six twin choke Weber fed, s.o.h.c. V12 former Alfa Romeo engineer Carlo Chiti had developed for the new formula. Chiti reverted to an s.o.h.c. head for less weight and complication and his version of the classic Colombo engine had individual rather than Siamesed intake ports. Chiti's 'Testa Rossa' (red head) engine was low stressed for its output but the car still relied upon drum brakes. The fastest works example in the hands of Collins/ Hawthorn struck clutch trouble early on and the problem eventually led to it being abandoned. The von Trips/Seidel car slid off at Indianapolis corner soon after half distance, having failed to keep the leader's pace. With rain set in, the race had been Gendebien/Hill versus Hamilton/ Bueb.

Jaguar was continuing to maintain a high profile thanks to a new 3.0 litre six derived from the regular 3.4. Equipped with carburettors, it was only rated at 254 b.h.p. Ecurie Ecosse had gone its own way with a bored and stroked 2.4 litre XK engine but both its entries fell out within the first half-an-hour: piston failure. However, the Hamilton car stayed around to take advantage of the overnight rain and, with the wet track lessening its power disadvantage, managed to overtake the leading Ferrari just before midnight. There wasn't really anything in it until the rain stopped at 2.00 a.m. The Ferrari had a one lap advantage at dawn...

But it wasn't over. Further rain increased Jaguar's chances. Alas, it all came to an unhappy ending shortly before midday – Hamilton went off the circuit avoiding an almost stationary back marker, an obstacle to which the spray had blinded him. His D-type ended upside down in a ditch.

Although none of the private Testa Rossas featured, Gendebien/Hill were there when it mattered, giving Ferrari its third Le Mans win. Having snatched the 1957 World Championship from Maserati (represented this year at Le Mans by one unsuccessful private entry), Ferrari was on the crest of a wave and seemingly destined for another title, in spite of the superior speed of the DBR1...

It was a bad race of the British marques. Only one Jaguar-powered car saw the finish, a Lister-Jaguar (Halford/Naylor) that ran in 15th but was unclassified, following camshaft and gearbox problems. The Lister was a successful 'special' in Britain and creator Brian Lister had sold a number of replicas for the '58 season. A second car run at Le Mans by the ENB registered an early retirement.

Early crashes eliminated two continental run D-types, those of Maurice Charles and Jean-Marie Brussin. Tragically, Brussin died as a consequence of injuries sustained after losing control under the Dunlop bridge and overturning the car.

The decimation of the ranks of British and Italian 3.0 litre prototypes left high pickings for the 2.0 litre runners. Fastest of these – and fourth quickest overall in practice – was the first 2.0 litre Lotus to be run at Le Mans. This light, mid-engined car was an early casualty piston failure, before it had been able to embarrass the 3.0 litre runners. There were five less competitive cars with 2.0 litre engines (two ACs, a Ferrari, a Maserati and a Peerless) but at the end of the day a little 1500cc Porsche bored out to 1600cc won the 2.0 litre class by a country mile. But for brake problems it might well have beaten the private Aston Martin into second... This race was another tribute to the excellence of the little German spyders, sister cars collecting fourth (first in 1500cc class) and fifth overall, ahead of two Testa Rossa stragglers. If the Ferrari and Aston Martin works teams couldn't find better form the following year, those strong, silver spyders might become an even greater embarrassment...

1.	3.0 Ferrari* (Gendebien/Hill)	5.	1.5 Porsche (de Beaufort/Linge)
2.	3.0 Aston Martin (Whitehead/Whitehead)	6.	3.0 Ferrari (Beurlys/de Changy)
3.	1.5 Porsche* (Behra/Herrmann)		* Class winners. Also:
4.	1.6 Porsche* (Barth/Frere)	11.	0.7 Osca (de Tomaso/Davis)

1959

It was a classic case of the hare and the tortoise and Aston Martin's finest hour.

After the disappointment of 1958, David Brown had given priority to a fledgling Grand Prix programme, with the exception of Le Mans. For this attempt the regular DBR1 would be aired, the policy one of preparation for reliability rather than development in search of more speed. That was all very well, but at the newly instigated Spring test weekend the latest version Testa Rossa lapped some 18 seconds quicker than the DBR1 – and both British cars present were in and out of the pits with worrying frequency. Ferrari had got around to disc brakes some six years late. The '59 Testa Rossa additionally benefited from a new Pinin Farina body shape and coil valve springs for higher r.p.m.

Aston Martin reacted to the lessons of the test weekend with revised aerodynamics: a plastic cover over the passenger seat, a revised tail and fared-in wheels were evident DBR1 modifications. In 24-hour trim the differential between the 270 b.h.p. British car and its 300 b.h.p. Italian rival had narrowed considerably...

Aston Martin pinned its hopes on the rivalry evident within the Ferrari team. Its own drivers were cool and highly experienced and agreed to divide any prize money among themselves in equal shares. The line-up was Salvadori/Shelby and Frere/Trintignant in regular seven-bearing engined cars and Moss/Fairman with a new four-bearing engine with higher compression ratio, offering an extra 10 b.h.p.

Moss's role was to draw the Testa Rossas into trouble and he duly shot into the lead, pursued by the works Ferraris of Gendebien/Hill and Allison/da Silva Ramos. A third example crewed by Behra/Gurney had been reluctant to fire up and Behra finished the first lap 15th. But the V12 car's temperament had really wound him up. By the end of the first hour he had sliced through to second spot and 20 minutes later he was past Moss and away, with a new 3.0 litre record in his pocket. Gurney continued the command but before dusk the car had run into trouble.

And so had the less highly-stressed examples, that of Allison/da Silva Ramos falling out altogether.

Amid Testa Rossa problems Moss/Fairman had gone back into the lead, but by the time Moss was into his second stint the engine had gone flat. An inlet valve had broken.

Behra/Gurney emerged in front once more, chased by a lone D-type (Ireland/Gregory) and the surviving Aston Martins. The Ferrari hit electrical problems as night drew in and the Jaguar's engine went sick.

Aston Martin was first and second...

Ferrari had lost two cars but Hill/Gendebien were still circulating and by 2.00 a.m. had overhauled the British runners. At half distance they were three laps to the good, comfortably outpacing the seven-bearing DBR1s, which continued the policy of 'slowly, slowly catchee monkey'...

As the final quarter of the race unfolded it seemed inevitable that the quicker Testa Rossa would win, but after its 11.00 a.m. stop the car was seen to be circulating slowly: it had terminal overheating...

Aston Martin's only worry now was to keep its cars properly paced – there was no challenge in sight... Salvadori/Shelby duly led Trintignant/Frere home by less than a lap to complete a great triumph for stamina over speed.

The victorious Aston Martins were the only survivors of 14 3.0 litre prototypes, the line-up having included a private Testa Rossa, a customer DBR1 and six Jaguar-engined machines. Of course, reliability had for so long been Jaguar's trump card but the race served only to confirm that the 3.0 litre version of the classic six did not have 24-hour staying power. Ecurie Ecosse ran three cars, that Ireland/Gregory D-type plus a Lister and a Tojeiro special. All three retired with engine failure, as did two works Listers and another customer Lister.

The list of 2.0 litre prototypes was similarly decimated: eight of nine, including two 1600cc works Porsches and a works V6 Ferrari, ran into trouble. The eventual demise of the 1600cc and 1500cc factory Porsches left the way open for strong finishes by GT cars and for the 2.0 litre prototype honours to go to a privately entered AC-Bristol. Using the same engine as had powered the third place Frazer Nash in the 1949 race, the AC Ace had been given its Le Mans debut in 1957 by Ken Rudd. Its simple, light Tojeiro-designed chassis and venerable six-cylinder engine had proved good enough for second in class. In 1958 two works cars had finished eighth and ninth overall. The '59 survivor claimed seventh overall.

1959 was the first year in which specific classes had been run for GT cars and Ferrari had responded with six 250 GTs, which were opposed by a single works Aston Martin DB4. The former used a milder version of the Testa Rossa V12, the latter a short stroke version of the 3.7 engine previously seen in the DBR2. This particular contest went in favour of Ferrari: Beurlys/Dernier led a procession that filled out the top six. Some consolation for Ferrari. With Aston Martin tiring of racing, the Italian marque was in the process of taking a firm grip on prototype *and* GT competition...

1.	3.0 Aston Martin* (Salvadori/Shelby)	6. 3.0 Ferrari (Fayen/Munaron)
2.	3.0 Aston Martin (Trintignant/Frere)	* Class winners. Also:
3.	3.0 Ferrari* (Beurlys/Elde)	7. 2.0 AC-Bristol (Whiteaway/Turner)
4.	3.0 Ferrari (Pilette/Arents)	8. 1.2 Lotus (Lumsden/Riley)
5.	3.0 Ferrari (Tavano/Grossmann)	9. 0.7 DB-Panhard (Cornet/Cotton)

1960

With the withdrawal of the works Aston Martin team (which had won the 1959 World Championship) Ferrari would have had a stranglehold on prototype racing, had it not been for the efforts of Giulio Alfrieri and 'Lucky' Casner.

Racing was in Maserati's blood. Not even poor financial health could keep it out entirely. During the difficult days of '58 when the state had been forced to move in to salvage the company, engineer Alfrieri had turned his attention to the conception of a new customer car to be powered by the marque's existing 2.0 litre straight four. Alfrieri was an admirer of the D-type's monocoque chassis but didn't feel he was in a position to exploit such technology: instead, he developed a practical but very stiff spaceframe constructed from around 200 short lengths of tube for his 'Birdcage' privateer car.

Born in 1959, the *Tipo* 60 had its modified 200SI four canted over, Mercedes-style, for a low bonnet line, independent front suspension, de Dion rear end as used by the last Maserati 250F Grand Prix cars, and disc brakes. From the USA came orders and pressure for a 3.0 litre engine.

Alfredi enlarged the 200SI to 2890cc and power went from 200 to 250 b.h.p.: 50 short of the Testa Rossa, perhaps, but the four cylinder Maserati had a 100kg weight advantage. American enthusiast Lucky Casner put together a works supported team to tackle the 1960 World Championship – the 'Camoradi' squad. Run by novices but funded by Goodyear and utilising the services of drivers of the calibre of Moss and Gurney, the team led the first three rounds of the five-event title chase with ease, only for its cars to break. However, round four at the Nurburgring was fourth time lucky.

For the Le Mans finale Alfrieri designed a more streamlined front end (with long windscreen gently raked from the front axle line) and longer tail. The novel windscreen helped the lead Gregory/Daigh entry set the Mulsanne pace. A new regulation having demanded a 10″ high windscreen on all prototypes, the Testa Rossa's conventional upright 'screen cut its top speed to around 160 m.p.h. Gregory/Daigh went 169 m.p.h. They were backed up by Munaron/Scarlatti in a *Tipo* 61 with standard front but long tail and by Casner/Jeffords in a completely standard example.

Gregory led from the start, with ease. The Testa Rossa was five seconds a lap slower. Ferrari had four works cars but two ran out of fuel just before the first scheduled stops. Then the day turned sour for

Many of the biggest engined cars in the 1960 race were GT machines: here an Ecurie Ecosse D-type beats Cunningham's Corvette off the line, while 3.0 litre sports-prototypes attempt to gain ground from further down the line. Photo: LAT.

Maserati. Before the end of the second hour the Gregory car became stuck in the pits, its starter motor faulty. The problem would cost an hour. The race fell into Ferrari hands.

Any hope left for Maserati died during the third hour when Munaron pulled off the track in response to smoke coming from the engine bay and found he could not re-start. His starter motor was burned out.

After a 25 minute starter motor switch, Casner put the third car into the sand and the sand jammed the gear selection mechanism. Meanwhile the streamliner had restarted, only to retire with a blown engine, just prior to midnight.

Maserati's demise left Gendebien/Frere leading Mairesse/Ginther and the private Testa Rossa of Rodriguez/Pilette. The works had entered two cars with familiar de Dion axles plus two with independent rear suspension using coil springs on a shorter frame. The all-independent TRI60 came out 50kgs lighter. Both models had dry sumped engine sitting lower in the car and new four-speed transmission. But the higher windscreen cut five seconds per lap and left the red prototypes struggling to outpace Maranello's 270 b.h.p. 250 GTs on the Mulsanne.

This year's team featured more experienced drivers, Le Mans veterans who were careful to stress their cars as little as possible in practice. April test day consumption checks had suggested 24 to 25 laps between fuel stops. Gendebien had pulled out of second place after 22 laps with the car spluttering from fuel shortage, probably as a consequence of fitting shorter exhausts since April. Frere had gone out again to see von Trip's similar TR60 and Scarfiotti's TRI60 stranded out on the circuit, tanks dry...

Overnight Gendebien/Frere held a narrow advantage over the Mairesse/Ginther TRI60 and the private TR60. At one stage the private car was passed by the private Aston Martin DBR1 of Clark/Salvadori but

it proved able to put the British car back in its place without too much effort. Only a u.j. failure on the surviving TRI60 cost Ferrari a clean sweep of the top three positions.

The Aston Martin privateer effort simply didn't have the pace of the works Ferraris. Although, after the 1959 Le Mans race, Aston Martin had found itself only two points behind Ferrari in the world title chase and had gone on to win the Goodwood TT to claim the crown, due to pressure of production car work it had been forced to announce its withdrawal from the sports car racing arena, at the same time giving its Grand Prix car one final season before it became obsolete through the impending 1.5

Gregory's Maserati Birdcage was the fastest car in the early stages of the 1960 race, but it was soon afflicted by a jammed starter... Photo: LAT.

litre Formula One. Alas, the 1960 Grand Prix effort was going from bad to worse, so the efforts of Border Reivers and Ian Ballie came as a welcome distraction. The Clark/Salvadori Reivers car led at the start, only for Clark to be passed by the Italian prototypes on the Mulsanne. However, he didn't fall far behind and at midnight the DBR1 lay third overall, two laps down and ahead of Rodriguez/Pilette, its progress aided by torrential rain which had given its crew a chance to harry the second-place factory Testa Rossa.

On Sunday the circuit was dry and the game DBR1 fell 11 laps adrift of the winning Ferrari to collect third place. The delayed Ian Ballie car (Ballie/Fairman) came home eighth overall.

Jaguar had nothing to show from its pair of private entries. Ecurie Ecosse's D-type (Flockhart/Bueb) shadowed the Scottish Aston Martin but retired at 5.30 a.m. with a broken crank. Less long-lived was the more interesting entry, the car which had been destined to take over from the D-type had the works continued in racing. 'E2A' had been designed in the mid-Fifties and boasted longer wheelbase, narrower track, revised aerodynamics and independent coil sprung rear suspension. A new alloy block fuel injected version of the 3.0 litre six endowed it with a healthy 290 b.h.p. but the scales told of a 30kgs weight penalty compared to the D-type. Borrowed by Briggs Cunningham and driven by Gurney/Hansgen, E2A ran with the Testa Rossas in the early laps but was soon in the pits with injection problems, which continued to bug it until its 1.40 a.m. demise due to head gasket failure.

A more successful British car was the MGA TC which won the 2.0 litre prototype class, in 12th position overall. The high places behind the 3.0 litre prototypes filling the top three slots were collected by GT runners. Ferrari had the unlimited capacity GT class to itself. Its latest short wheelbase 250 GT had Testa Rossa heads and examples took fourth, fifth, sixth and seventh overall, ahead of the survivor of the four-strong Camoradi/Cunningham-entered, works-assisted Chevrolet Corvette entry. Cunningham/Kimberley crashed, Thompson/Windridge's 4.6 litre V8 blew up and Lilley/Gamble were unclassified, but the names of Fitch and Grossman were inscribed on the results list. The class-winning Ferrari was in the hands of Tavano/Loustel. The previous year's class winner, Beurlys, crashed during Saturday's storm. So Ferrari had filled five of the top six positions. Was Le Mans to become its private race in this new decade?

1.	3.0 Ferrari* (Gendebien/Frere)		* Class winners. Also:
2.	3.0 Ferrari (Rodriguez/Pilette)	8.	4.6 Chevrolet (Fitch/Grossmann)
3.	3.0 Aston Martin (Clark/Salvadori)	10.	1.6 Porsche (Linge/Walter)
4.	3.0 Ferrari* (Tavano/Loustel)	12.	1.8 MG (Lund/Escott)
5.	3.0 Ferrari (Arents/Connell)	13.	1.2 Lotus (Masson/Laurent)
6.	3.0 Ferrari (Elde/Noblet)	15.	0.7 DB-Panhard (Laureau/Armagnac)
		16.	1.0 Austin-Healey (Dalton/Colgate)

1961

It was another Ferrari race, but a very significant one for it ushered in a new technology: the big capacity, mid-engined prototype. Porsche had long used a central engine location for its successful small capacity prototypes and Cooper and Lotus had proven the advantages of the layout in Grand Prix racing. Smaller frontal area, light weight and useful weight distribution had endowed their all-independently-sprung chassis with sufficient performance to offset the poor power output of their small, light four-cylinder engines on 'handling' courses. The switch to a 1.5 litre formula for 1961 had made the mid-engined layout *de rigueur* for Grand Prix racing and Lotus had already shown that a 2.0 litre mid-engined prototype could be very competitive, even at Le Mans. In 1961 Maserati put its faith in the concept for a 3.0 litre car, while Cooper and Ferrari weighed in with 2.5 litre machines.

Ferrari considered its Testa Rossa V12 engine too long for an effective mid-engine chassis and built an experimental machine with V6 behind the driver, instead. This was the 246SP with the 2471cc, 60 degree V6 seen in the front of the 1960 Ferrari Grand Prix car. It was a d.o.h.c., dry sump engine which, breathing through three Webers, produced 270 b.h.p. (an excellent 112 per litre). It nestled in an enclosed wheel version of the latest mid-engined 1.5 litre Formula One car developed by Chiti, with independent suspension front and rear and characteristic 'twin nostril' nose.

Alfrieri's mid-engined car was a direct development of the existing four cylinder *Tipo* 61 'Birdcage', the model rebuilt around the new engine location with independent rear suspension. For Le Mans the revamped *Tipo* 63 was equipped with an enlarged version of the marque's 2.5 litre V12 Grand Prix engine, the four cylinder having been a disappointment in early races...

The opening round of the 1961 title chase at Sebring had been won by the '61 Testa Rossa, which boasted a more aerodynamic body, Chiti having convinced Ferrari of the need to cheat the wind. The qualified aerodynamicist had even managed to get a wind tunnel installed at Maranello. He had given the Testa Rossa a 'roofless coupé' look with reprofiled nose, more steeply raked screen and higher tail, cut off in 'Kamm' style.

The 246SP looked similar and caused a stir by winning the second 1961 World Championship race, the Targa Florio. And then the front-engined *Tipo* 61 Maserati had repeated its 'Ring triumph. Three pre-Le

The Gendebien/Hill front engined V12 Ferrari leads the Ginther/von Trips mid engined V6 Ferrari onto another lap. The 3.0 litre V12 car was fast and reliable enough to win the 1961 race but the 2.4 litre V6 machine pointed the way to the future. Photo: LAT.

Mans Championship races, three very different results.

Alfrieri put all his faith in the mid-engined V12 car for Le Mans. Casner's four had won the German race but the factory had fallen out with his Camoradi team, which had lost its Goodyear backing. Two of the three V12s entered were allocated to Cunningham, the other to the Italian Serenissima team. They were not successful. Hansgen got his Cunningham car up to third early on, only to crash in drizzle which arrived in the third hour. The other cars were plagued by overheating. However, Thompson/ Pabst made it through to fourth place, behind a GT Ferrari, in the second Cunningham entry. Without a doubt Maserati would have done better by sticking to four cylinders and a front engine. A back-up 2.0 litre '60 entered by Cunningham ran steadily to eighth overall, third in the 2.0 litre class.

Whereas the mid-engined Maseratis did not have staying power and the 2.5 litre Cooper Monaco was another victim of the early drizzle, the 246SP caused another stir by running strongly with the leading Testa Rossas, in spite of its power disadvantage. Driven by Ginther/von Trips, its surprising run lasted 16 hours, then it ran out of fuel...

So this Ferrari race belonged to the old generation. But the winning Testa Rossa was notable for its more aerodynamic shape, which culminated in a 'spoiler'. Ginther is credited with the discovery that a strip of metal across the back of the car to 'spoil' the flow off the rear deck could provide a useful measure of rear end downforce, increasing cornering stability and grip.

The front-engined factory cars were handled by Gendebien/Hill and Mairesse/Parkes and again it was Gendebien who came through to win, although this year Mairesse survived to claim second. The position which rightly belonged to the Rodriguez brothers' NART-entered ex-works Testa Rossa. It had duelled with the winning car for much of the night and, despite losing 20 minutes to an ignition problem at 7.00 a.m., had looked set for second – until at 2.00 p.m. a piston cried enough.

With Maserati's demise, it had been left to Aston Martin privateers to chase the fast Ferraris, in the absence of any Jaguars. Again, two DBR1s ran, one in the colours of John Ogier's Essex Racing Team (Salvadori/Maggs), the other fielded by Border Reivers (Clark/Flockhart). The former looked set to finish runner-up to the successful Ferraris (the swifter similar car having fallen out), when it succumbed to a leaking fuel tank on Sunday morning.

Both examples had suffered the humiliation of running behind the fastest GT car, a rapid Ferrari 250 in the hands of Moss/Hill G., which fell out early on Sunday morning after providing splendid support for the Ferrari prototypes. Its demise handed third place to a more subdued 250 GT (Noblet/Guichet), the marque overcoming three privately entered Aston Martin DB4s to claim the GT honours, even if only two of eight runners lasted. Among Ferrari's GT retirements was an experimental factory car, a lightweight short wheelbase model with special body by Pinin Farina and 300 b.h.p. Testa Rossa engine. Driven by Tavano/Baghetti, engine problems cost it a high finish soon after half distance.

Splitting the surviving Ferrari GT cars (third and sixth) were the troubled Maserati and a 2.0 litre class-winning Porsche prototype driven by Gregory/Holbert, Porsche again dominating both 2.0 litre and 1500cc classes. After so much success for the little silver cars, the Ferrari 246 SP had at last suggested that a mid-engined prototype could be a realistic proposition for outright honours. Front-engined Ferraris had now equalled Jaguar's five-win record: what price success for mid-engined Ferraris?

1.	3.0 Ferrari* (Gendebien/Hill)	6.	3.0 Ferrari (Grossmann/Pilette)
2.	3.0 Ferrari (Mairesse/Parkes)		* Class winners. Also:
3.	3.0 Ferrari* (Noblet/Guichet)	10.	1.6 Porsche (Linge/Pon)
4.	3.0 Maserati (Pabst/Thompson)	12.	1.2 Lotus (Allen/Taylor)
5.	2.0 Porsche* (Gregory/Holbert)	14.	0.8 Fiat Abarth (Hulme/Hyslop)

1962

1962 was to have been the year of the GT car. The CSI had announced that prototypes were to be cast aside, that it would award its World titles to three categories of GT car (up to 1000cc – to 2500cc – to 4000cc). However, the organisers of the classic endurance races didn't want to lose the spectacle of the prototypes. The ACO combined with the organisers of the Sebring 12-hours, the Targa Florio and the 'Ring 1000kms, to stage their own 'World Challenge of Speed and Endurance' for 'experimental' cars up to 4.0 litres, arguing that there had to be some way for manufacturers to develop future GT cars. This gave Ferrari an excuse to continue its mid-engined prototype programme and a 246 SP won both the Targa Florio and the 'Ring 1000kms. However, at La Sarthe the machine would face bigger capacity 'experimental' opposition – 4.0 litre front-engined coupés from Maserati and Aston Martin. Ferrari replied with a 4.0 litre 'experimental' car of its own – like the 246 SP, less in the spirit of experimental *GT* cars than the offerings from the rival marques: an independently sprung Testa Rossa chassis with big bore long stroke version of the familiar V12 displacing 3968cc and producing in excess of 350 b.h.p. The return to the Big Banger Le Mans prototype ...

The one-off Ferrari ran on big, 16″ wheels and had a modified tail sporting a wide 'aerodynamic' roll bar which deflected air towards the rear spoiler. With as much as 390 b.h.p. going through the standard Testa

Ferrari's idea of an 'Experimental' car in the Year of the GT Machine was this 4.0 litre Testa Rossa which Hill/Gendebien had only to conduct carefully to ensure victory. Photo: LAT.

The agile '246SP' mid engined V6 Ferrari prototype of the Rodriguez brothers kept the winning Ferrari Testa Rossa close company in the first half of the 1962 race, in spite of a 1.6 litre capacity disadvantage. Photo: LAT.

Rossa transmission, the drivers would need a light, careful touch and two experienced endurance men were chosen: Gendebien and Hill.

The 4.0 litre prototype was the fastest machine at the circuit and was driven as slowly as possible to win. In the early stages the 4.0 litre Maserati and Aston Martin coupés kept it close company. With these four challengers having hit trouble by nightfall, its little mid-engined V6 stablemate in the hands of the Rodriguez brothers kept it from getting lonely. Indeed, the 246 SP traded the lead until it broke its transmission, around half distance. Thereafter, the potent Testa Rossa's cruise home was spoiled only by clutch bothers which loomed at 10.00 a.m. Nevertheless, by this stage it was under no pressure at all and could be driven ever more gingerly.

Early in the course of its winning gait the long stroke front-engined car had broken the five-year-old lap record set by Hawthorn in a 4.5 litre Maranello machine, with a careful lap two seconds slower than its practice best.

The demise of the V6 mid-engined sports racer handed second spot to a similar car handled by Baghetti/Scarfiotti, one equipped with Ferrari's first-ever V8 engine, a Chiti-designed 2645cc s.o.h.c. unit producing something less than the 275 b.h.p. of the smaller V6. Seemingly, therefore, rather pointless in view of the V8 unit's greater weight and length. But not if one considers it as an experimental device – a step towards putting the even heavier, even longer V12 behind the driver...

Alas, the V8 car eventually went the way of the V6 machine, due to gearbox failure after 17 hours. Two conventional (3.0 litre) Testa Rossas also expired, so 'experimental' cars became rather thin on the ground. Another in trouble was Ferrari's pure experimental *GT*: a modified 250 GT chassis with the 4.0 litre Testa Rossa engine. This device was forced into a sandbank during the pushing and shoving of the opening laps and subsequently retired with overheating.

Aston Martin's 330 b.h.p. 'experimental' GT car fared little better, although it caused raised eyebrows by running with Gendebien/Hill in the early laps. Indeed, Aston Martin's dealer pressure influenced works racing return got off to a great start with this DB4 GT-based 'Project 212' aerodynamic coupé (using the '57 3.7 litre alloy six bored to 4.0 litres) leading during the first round of pit stops. It was lying in second spot during the second hour when a dynamo change bugged its progress but continued to run strongly in the hands of Hill G./Ginther until an internal oil pump failure spelt retirement at 10.00 p.m.

By that stage Maserati's three '*Tipo* 151' GT coupé-bodied 'experimental' cars had all hit trouble. Reverting to a front-engined layout (like Ferrari, Maserati was now wary of a big engine behind the driver), the new coupé utilised a 4.0 litre version of the old Birdcage 450S engine. The chassis had a more straightforward frame than the cars but with 360 b.h.p. on tap this 'GT' device could top 180 m.p.h. on the Mulsanne. Alas, Trintignant/Bianchi (Maserati France) struck a bank and withdrew in the face of abnormal tyre wear, Kimberley/Thompson (Cunningham) crashed out and McLaren/Hansgen (Cunningham) lost time to rear tyre trouble. Not that the trio had ever been a cause of worry for the Ferrari demonstrators. Cunningham's surviving entry was destined to retire from fifth place at 5.00 a.m. with a burned piston.

With all but one of the fast 'experimental' cars falling by the wayside, the road was left clear for a World Championship title chasing GT car to finish second – and this honour went to yet another Ferrari. The Maranello marque had produced an aerodynamic version of the 250 GT powered by the dry sump 3.0 litre Testa Rossa engine. It was dubbed 'GTO' and was run by privateers. Six customer cars faced three lightweight 3.8 litre Jaguar E Types and a pair of 3.7 litre Aston Martin DB4 GTs. Both Aston Martins blew up but two of the Jaguars saw the finish, beaten only by two of the six GTOs.

In winning GT, Noblet/Guichet finished less than 45 miles behind the carefully paced overall winner, having enjoyed a troublefree run. Elde/Buerlys similarly encountered no problems, moving into a solid third place overall with a few hours to run as the Lumsden/Sargent E-type fell back with transmission bothers, behind the sister Cunningham car of Cunningham/Salvadori. Sixth was another GTO, a NART entry (Grossman/Roberts).

So, although Ferrari filled four of the top six places, Jaguar was once again prominent in the final classification, thanks to the new importance of GT racing, which had tempted the marque back. The factory had a design for a new prototype, but what future had prototypes?

1.	4.0 Ferrari* (Hill/Gendebien)			* Class winners. Also:
2.	3.0 Ferrari* (Noblet/Guichet)		7.	1.6 Porsche (Barth/Herrmann)
3.	3.0 Ferrari (Elde/Beurlys)		8.	1.2 Lotus (Hobbs/Gardner)
4.	3.8 Jaguar (Cunningham/Salvadori)		13.	2.0 Morgan (Lawrence/Shepherd-Barron)
5.	3.8 Jaguar (Sargent/Lumsden)		16.	0.7 Panhard (Bertaut/Guilhaudin)
6.	3.0 Ferrari (Grossmann/Roberts)		17.	1.0 Bonnet (Consten/Rosinski)

1963

If the CSI had allowed sports car racing to get into a muddle in 1962, its changes for the new season did little to salvage the situation. While continuing to award World Championship titles to three classes of homologated GT car, it put up an additional World Trophy for *Prototypes GT*. Although it was clearly intended that this legalisation of the World Challenge for Speed and Endurance should cater for GT development cars, there were no rules to exclude pure prototypes. Nor was there a capacity limit. Only established GT manufacturers could field 'Prototype GT' cars. For them it was an official return to unlimited capacity prototype racing, six years on...

At Maranello a 'prototype' was a pure mid-engined racing car and the ruling marque continued its mid-engined prototype programme with gusto. By 1963 it had resolved itself to the idea of putting a V12 behind the driver and the Testa Rossa engine found its way into a wider track, longer wheelbase version of the V6/V8 chassis, sporting more conventional nose and the 4.0 litre Testa Rossa's 'aerodynamic roll bar'. The result was good handling and grip plus a reliable 310 b.h.p. from the slightly improved 3.0 litre engine. The only drawback of the new '250P' was a 100kg weight penalty compared with the V6 car. It was unusual for its placement of the clutch behind the gearbox.

With good power and excellent cornering, there was nothing to beat Ferrari's 1963 prototype at Le Mans. Maserati and Aston Martin countered with improved versions of their '62 'experimental' coupés but in the 250P the front-engined sports car had met its match. The sleek Zagato-bodied, tubular frame 'Project 214' Aston Martin sat its engine 200mm further back in the chassis, had independent rear suspension and a rear mounted five-speed gearbox. Its record 187 m.p.h. Mulsanne speed was impressive, as was its second row grid position. It even had a moment of glory, leading under the Dunlop bridge on lap one. As the race settled down it kept in touch but no sooner had Hill handed to Bianchi than a driveshaft broke, the legacy of hitting accident debris.

The *Tipo* 151 owned by Colonel Simone of Maserati France had been rebuilt on a shorter wheelbase and now had a de Dion rear axle and new 5.0 litre d.o.h.c. engine based on the production 5000GT's V8, which provided the sheer speed to worry the 250P. It lacked the stamina. For two hours Simon/Casner kept the Ferraris company. No sooner had the more sophisticated machines drawn out an advantage than the gallant challenger broke its gearbox.

Start of the 1963 race with the now NART-run, '62-winning, front engined Ferrari getting away ahead of the mid engined Ferrari that was destined to scoop the honours this year. Car No. 18 is the Project 214 Aston. Photo: LAT.

Up front were Surtees/Mairesse, followed by Parkes/Maglioli. The third 250P of Bandini/Scarfiotti was following the '62 winning 4.0 litre Testa Rossa, now owned by NART and entrusted to Rodriguez P./Penske. Alas, by 10.00 p.m. the American entry had fallen to tenth place having lost a number of treads (it was not using the traditional Dunlop covers). Later it broke an oil pipe...

The 250P trio lost formation towards 11.00 p.m., the Parkes/Maglioli car suffering ignition trouble which took a while to diagnose. It fell to 17th position. Over the next 12 hours it steadily regained ground while its sister cars reigned majestically at the front of the field. Surtees/Mairesse built a two-lap cushion but, with less than six hours to run, their car caught fire at the Esses as a fuel spillage was ignited by an exhaust blow-back. Brim full of fuel, the 250P burst into flames. The Belgian suffered slight burns. Parkes/Maglioli eventually drew up into second place, but with less than an hour to go lapsed onto 11 cylinders and fell behind the leading GT car, a GTO.

New technology leads old in '63 – the Surtees/Mairesse 250P leads the Rodriguez/Penske Testa Rossa. The 250P gave away one litre but gained extra cornering ability through its mid engine placement. Photo: LAT.

Ferrari won GT in the face of sterner opposition. Indeed, the charismatic GTO even humbled the marque's genuine Prototype (GT), the 330 LMB – a marriage of 4.0 litre Testa Rossa engine and lengthened Berlinetta Lusso production chassis. Three of these creations, less sophisticated but more powerful than the GTO, were entered via private teams but only one finished, the carefully conducted Maranello Concessionaires (GB) example (Sears/Salmon) which finished fifth.

The homologated GT ranks saw four GTOs face three Cunningham-entered lightweight E-types, two factory DB4 GTs plus one private example, the two Ford-backed, works-entered, 4.7 litre Ford pushrod V8-powered Shelby/AC Cobras (taking advantage of the abolition of a maximum capacity limit for homologated GT cars).

One of the American-run Coventry Cats was an early retirement with a broken gearbox and a sister car was soon in the pits with transmission trouble. Later both survivors crashed but one of them, handled by Cunningham himself, made it home, if well out of the reckoning following extensive accident repairs.

Aston Martin lost all its cars, two to blown engines, the other to an overheating rear axle. However, the McLaren/Ireland DB4 GT had been leading the GT runners when its engine had expired, after five hours.

The Cobras, based on a coil sprung version of the AC Ace chassis and good for 380 b.h.p., were not so fleet, lacking Mulsanne pace, but at least the team brought one home in seventh place. This was a learning year for the new American-inspired challenge, as yet no great threat to the GTO horde.

By half distance Ferrari's force had a stranglehold on the big capacity GT class, its three representatives holding third, fourth and fifth overall. The car running third, a NART entry (Piper/Gregory) boasted a special, sleek Pinin Farina body. Sadly, burned out dynamo bushes, then an 'off'

Car of the future. The Lola GT that appeared in 1963 was the mid engined, monocoque chassis forerunner of the GT40. Photo: LAT.

dropped it to sixth at the finish. Two 250 GTOs entered by ENB had far less trouble and wound up sandwiching the sick 250P, Beurlys/von Ophem claiming the honour of second overall.

Also having cause to celebrate was the Rover-BRM team, which accepted the ACO's challenge to run a turbine-powered car at an average speed in excess of 150 k.p.h. and achieved a splendid 173.546 k.p.h. in scooping the 'Special Award'. Its runner was based on a BRM Formula One chassis and a light Rover gas turbine engine. The turbine produced in the region of 150 b.h.p. but had to be kept spinning at 35/40000 r.p.m., even while cornering, so the drivers were thankful there weren't too many sharp bends.

While some suggested the turbine might be the engine of the future (the Rover finished an unofficial eighth overall), a more realistic picture of the prototype of tomorrow was painted by a works Lola GT coupé powered by a 4.2 litre Ford pushrod. Lola's Eric Broadley had produced the first serious mid-engined monocoque prototype. The pretty coupé-bodied Lola, which didn't feature due to dynamo and transmission troubles, not to mention a dire lack of development time, ended up a wreck. However, its chassis construction was far ahead of the 250P and its designer was destined to play a very significant role in the future of the Le Mans prototype...

1.	3.0 Ferrari* (Scarfiotti/Bandini)		* Class winners. Also:
2.	3.0 Ferrari* (Beurlys/Langlois)	7.	4.7 AC-Ford (Bolton/Sanderson)
3.	3.0 Ferrari (Parkes/Maglioli)	8.	2.0 Porsche (Barth/Linge)
4.	3.0 Ferrari (Elde/Dumay)	9.	3.8 Jaguar (Richards/Grossmann)
5.	4.0 Ferrari* (Sears/Salmon)	10.	1.2 Lotus (Wagstaff/Fergusson)
6.	3.0 Ferrari (Gregory/Piper)	11.	1.1 Bonnet (Beltoise/Bobrowski)

1964

Early in 1963 Henry Ford had gone to the Sebring 12-Hours to see Carroll Shelby's Ford-financed Cobras trounce the opposition. To his consternation they hadn't done so. Ferrari had got in the way. 'Let's buy those fast little red cars,' is said to have been his reaction...

Serious negotiations between Ford and Ferrari did subsequently take place. The failure of Ford's 1963 buy-out bid presented Ferrari with a massive threat to both its GT and prototype campaigns. Ford was in the midst of a 'Total Performance' programme aimed at increasing its youth appeal through racing. Victory at Le Mans was made high priority. The Cobra was readied for an all-out attack on the GT crown and Ford developed its own prototype in conjunction with Lola.

Ford enlisted the services of Aston Martin competitions director John Wyer and Lola's Eric Broadley who, in line with design studies produced by Ford Engineering (USA) under Roy Lunn, from mid '63 presided over the creation of a more heavily engineered derivative of his '62-designed Lola GT. Len Bailey played a major role in the detail design.

The Ford GT40 featured a steel monocoque incorporating a box section sponson either side of the cockpit housing the fuel tanks and an integral roof and windscreen surround. Independent wishbone suspension was hung from sub frames either end and the sponsons extended back to help support the engine. The aerodynamics had been devised using scale models in Ford's Dearborn, Michigan, wind tunnel and the wide, road-car-style cockpit canopy showed the influence of Ford's regular stylists.

Unveiled early in '64, the hurriedly built GT40's power plant was a Fairline-based alloy 4.2 litre pushrod V8 developed for Indianapolis. Fed petrol through four Webers, the dry sump unit produced around 350 b.h.p. (less than 75 per litre). It drove through a Colotti four-speed gearbox. Girling provided the disc brakes, Dunlop the tyres. The car first ran in public at the '64 Le Mans test weekend and Schlesser crashed heavily at the Mulsanne kink. An aerodynamic problem was diagnosed and the car looked a better bet on its race debut in the 'Ring 1000kms with prominent rear spoiler. Even if it did retire with broken suspension and its gearbox showing signs of imminent failure. It was only a year since Lunn

In spite of the arrival of the Ford GT40, Ferrari's mid engined prototype had the upper hand in 1964. However, it was clear that the American corporation would not be put off by failure on its first Le Mans attempt... Photo: LAT.

had instigated the first design studies, and only a couple of weeks before Le Mans . . .

The GT40 was fast in practice for Le Mans, reaching 191.4 m.p.h. on the Mulsanne and lapping almost four seconds quicker than the Lola GT had gone. Progress had been made but there was a crying lack of development time . . .

The car showed its hand on the second lap – the first had been led by three works Ferrari prototypes but Ginther went past them all on the Mulsanne and proceeded to pull away until his fuel stop at around the one-and-a-half-hour mark. Ford's hare relinquished the lead but after three hours co-driver Gregory was back in front. The car held sway until early in the fourth hour, when its transmission cried enough.

But the battle wasn't over yet. Attwood/Schlesser were well placed, driving a more circumspect race . . . until their GT40 caught fire in the sixth hour, apparently due to the use of an inadequate fuel hose. That left one last hope, Hill/McLaren, whose car had been delayed by carburation problems in the early laps and was gradually rising from 44th position at the end of the first hour. Its transmission held out until the 13th hour, at which stage it had risen to fourth place, making the fastest lap of the race in the process.

The demise of the blue and white runners left those red cars in charge again. A mildly modified Maserati 151 of Maserati France had been but a token effort (in spite of a 190 m.p.h. Mulsanne speed). It retired early through electrical failure. And this year Aston Martin was only represented in GT.

Ferrari had mustered quite a fleet to face the arrival of Ford. Into its 250P chassis, substantially unaltered, it had dropped a choice of bigger bore version of the 3.0 litre V12 displacing 3285cc and producing 320 b.h.p. or the 4.0 litre V12, now producing 370 b.h.p. In the former guise the car was known as the 275P, in the latter as the 330P, in which case it had 1″ wider rims. There were two 275Ps and three 330Ps present, two of

The Ford GT40 was too new realistically to hope to win in 1964, but the promise was there for all to see. Photo: LAT.

the latter in private hands (Maranello Concessionaires and NART). In addition, NART and the ENB each had another 3.3 litre prototype, the 275LM, which, although essentially a 250P, with roof and the enlarged engine was Ferrari's planned '64 GT car. However, Ferrari didn't have the anticipated homologation papers. It had merely a claim to have the parts and the intent to produce 100 examples...

Of the seven-strong Ferrari fleet, the 275s were reckoned to be the more dependable – the 330's torque was enough to make its transmission marginal. NART's 330P was an early retirement. The Maranello example ran into numerous snags and the pole position works example (Surtees/Bandini) lost a lot of time to a broken petrol pipe and a water leak. Both struggling examples lost compression overnight and the factory 275P of Vaccarella/Guichet got five laps ahead. This was the only 275 to finish strongly – accidents and oil pump and clutch problems afflicted the others, although the ENB car did see the finish, a lowly 16th.

So Ferrari collected the top three positions, ahead of the GT battle. Following the CSI's refusal to homologate the 275LM, Ferrari had developed a refined GTO with reshaped and lowered body, wider wheels and some engine refinements, four examples of which faced three Cobras, two lightweight E-types and a lone DB4 GT.

The Cobras of Gurney/Bondurant and Sears/Bolton quickly emerged as the fastest runners and the DB4 GT did a great job of keeping the GTOs out of the top three GT positions. However, the Aston Martin got disqualified for taking on oil. The third Cobra was another to infringe the rules. The AC Cars-entered Sears/Bolton coupé (with different aerodynamics to the two Shelby coupés) was delayed by a fuel system bug then crashed as a result of a tyre blow-out, but the remaining Shelby car ran on supremely as GT pace-setter. The GTO/64 got its only taste of leading while the American car had a leaking oil pipe fixed: the 380 b.h.p. American car was too fast for it. The Shelby American Inc. machine recovered to finish one lap ahead of the ENB's GTO, taking fourth place. The GTOs claimed fifth, sixth and ninth, NART's ninth-placed car having fallen back with a failing engine after heading the Ferrari GT runners overnight. The American team lost a second example to a blown rear axle.

Unwilling or unable to produce 100 examples of the 275LM, Ferrari was poised to follow Jaguar and Aston Martin out of GT racing. All effort at Maranello would have to be directed towards checking the growing Ford prototype threat.

1.	3.3 Ferrari* (Guichet/Vaccarella)	6.	3.0 Ferrari (Ireland/Maggs)
2.	4.0 Ferrari (Bonnier/Hill)		* Class winners. Also:
3.	4.0 Ferrari (Surtees/Bandini)	7.	2.0 Porsche (Buchet/Ligier)
4.	4.7 AC-Ford* (Gurney/Bondurant)	13.	1.6 Alfa Romeo (Businello/Deserti)
5.	3.0 Ferrari* (Bianchi/Beurlys)	14.	5.4 Iso Rivolta (Berney/Noblet)
		22.	1.2 Lotus (Hunt/Wagstaff)

1965

Ford did not progress properly from the promise of '64. For one thing, the company had too many chiefs on its prototype programme. For example, it wasn't clear as to whether it was intended for the car to be developed by Lunn or Broadley. Understandably, the experienced British race engineer became disenchanted and moved on elsewhere...

Equally as serious was pressure from within the organisation for quick results. Following the retirements of '64 (to which had been added three cars in the Rheims 12-Hour race) an alternative 'MkII' version had been developed, diverting attention from the quest to sort the standard car.

And although the standard GT40 had yet to find success, a decision had already been taken to homologate it for GT racing by producing 100 examples...

The MkII had mildly modified chassis and big 7.0 litre V8 developed by Ford's Kar Kraft Detroit subsidiary. Its race programme was put in the hands of Shelby American under Phil Remington while Wyer's UK-based Ford Advanced Vehicles (FAV) concentrated on the GT40 and its long build programme. Wyer switched it from the troublesome Colotti to a ZF gearbox. The wider track, Goodyear-shod chassis built for the MkII was equipped with a Ford Galaxie-based transmission.

The GT40 was switched from the alloy 4.2 V8 to a 4.7 litre iron block version of the same, as used in the Cobra. This heavier, wet sump '289' unit produced 380 b.h.p. and more torque while the dependable 7.0 litre NASCAR V8 – the iron block '427 wedge' engine – supplied 475 b.h.p. and produced massive torque to compensate for its puny 67 b.h.p. per litre and 70kg weight penalty. Although fitted with a dry sump, it was unsophisticated, using push rods and single (four barrel) Holley carburettor.

The MkII was no heavier than the rival 4.0 litre, 410 b.h.p. Ferrari prototypes and was fast, exceeding 200 m.p.h. on the Mulsanne. Like the GT40 the previous year, it lacked development. Shelby entered two examples, backed up by two Daytona Continental winning 4.7 GT40s. Singleton GT40 entries came from FAV and Ford France.

For sheer speed Ferrari had nothing to match the MkII's shattering 138.4 m.p.h. practice average; not even its new 4.0 litre car was that fast. This was Technical Director Mauro Forghieri's P2, featuring a new chassis having a spaceframe reinforced with alloy panels for extra rigidity, along the lines of Forghieri's contemporary Formula One cars.

Ford came back to Le Mans after its 'learning' year with a bigger engine, this unsophisticated 7.0 litre V8 stockblock. The so-equipped MkII, like the GT40 the previous year, lacked development time. Photo: LAT.

Like the Ford, it ran on cast rather than wire wheels equipped with (Dunlop) tubeless tyres. Its body shape was new and more slippery, although retaining the open cockpit and aerodynamic roll bar.

The chassis frame was not only reinforced around its central section, it also carried the latest Ferrari V12 as a highly stressed member. This was a new alloy engine, derived from the classic V12, with combined block and crankcase for additional rigidity. It introduced twin cam heads and was available in 3.3 and 4.0 litre versions, rated respectively at 350 and 410 b.h.p. The four cammers were not supplied to customers but for Maranello and NART the factory had a big bore 4.4 litre version of the regular s.o.h.c. V12, said to produce almost as much power as the new derivative.

The factory fielded two 330P2s and a 275P2, the latter equipped with a unique closed coupé body. In support were the 365P2s of the British and American teams (one apiece) and a pair of 275LMs from the same teams, plus a 275LM from the ENB.

With all that stirring machinery on hand (a total of 14 glory-seeking prototypes representing the two giants of the race), the race itself was an anti-climax. First, Maserati had its final fling. Siffert/Neerpasch had been entrusted with the latest (and last) '*Tipo* 65' sports racer from the proud factory. It was another 5.0 litre V8 car funded by Simone, this one rush-built in France. The design came from Alfrieri and featured spaceframe chassis with mid-engine location and GT-style coupé bodywork. It was not reputed to handle well and although it got away first it did not manage to stay on the track throughout the first lap...

The MkIIs were quickly into their stride but within three hours the big Ford challenge had collapsed. Ford France had been the first to go, losing its GT40 to transmission failure. Before two hours were up Shelby had lost its pair to head gasket failure. Soon afterwards, the hastily developed MkIIs had started to suffer, afflicted by all manner of ailments. Transmission failure was the eventual cause of retirement. The FAV GT40 became another victim of the 4.7 litre's head gasket curse after five hours, but Ford had lost face a couple of hours ago and by midnight had lost its last wounded MkII.

The Ford MkII made a fine sight in full flight but was not yet ready to upset a marque that had contested Le Mans since 1949... Photo: LAT.

But Ferrari wasn't to do much better. True, the P2s had been able to fill the first five places by the three-hour mark, taking a stranglehold on the race, but that grip would be broken... Only one of the P2s was destined to finish, and then only in seventh place.

At first it was cracked discs, a new ventilated type not standing up to the pounding of the Mulsanne corner after cooling along the straight. The causes of retirement were clutch and engine problems – probably resulting from the drivers having to compensate for deficient brakes. The only exception was the Maranello 365P2, which retired due to a broken exhaust manifold which was filling the cockpit with fumes! The British team also lost its 275LM, to transmission trouble, but the NART sister car came through to save the day for Ferrari after an epic journey.

The Rindt/Gregory-crewed car had suffered ignition trouble early on and had languished in 18th position at the four-hour mark. However, some inspired, never-say-die driving had seen it gradually reel in the ENB 275LM which had been left out front with the demise of the P2s. Rindt/Gregory relieved Dumay/Gosselin of the lead with less than four hours to run...

Third was the only traditional-style Ferrari in the race, a 275GTB – a production GT car that had been developed for its 24-hour stamina rather than its speed. It outlasted all the Cobras.

With the decimation of the big capacity runners, fourth and fifth places were filled by 2.0 litre class-winning Porsche 904 coupés, shrugging off a threat from the Rover-BRM. Absent from the '64 event, the turbine car was back under an equivalency ruling that nominated it as a 2.0 litre contender. This year it had uprated suspension, new bodywork and heat exchangers to produce greater power. Sadly the engine swallowed something which caused internal damage, leading to high exhaust temperatures. The fuel delivery rate had to be reduced as a consequence and the overall average speed fell by 9 m.p.h. compared with '63. The car fell to 10th overall.

Rover didn't have plans to be back, unlike Ford which had to shrug off the inevitable barrage of press criticism that followed in the wake of its Saturday debacle...

1.	3.3 Ferrari* (Rindt/Gregory)	6.	3.3 Ferrari (Spoerry/Boller)
2.	3.3 Ferrari (Dumay/Gosselin)		* Class winners. Also:
3.	3.3 Ferrari* (Mairesse/Beurlys)	7.	4.4 Ferrari (Rodriguez/Vaccarella)
4.	2.0 Porsche (Linge/Nocker)	9.	5.4 Iso Griffo (Fraissinet/de Mortemart)
5.	2.0 Porsche (Koch/Fischaber)	12.	1.3 Austin-Healey (Hawkins/Rhodes)
		13.	1.1 Triumph (Thuner/Lampinen)

1966

This had to be Ford's year. No expense was spared. The MkII that had shaken tarmac the previous year had re-appeared, better developed, to sweep the early season home races at Daytona and Sebring. No attempt was made to contest the subsequent European six-hour and 1000km World Championship events. All effort was saved for Le Mans. The company applied for no less than *15* starting places to be filled by 7.0 litre prototypes, to be granted an awesome eight. The cars were to be run by Shelby (three), NASCAR team Holman Moody (three) and the British outfit Alan Mann Racing. With stronger monocoque to cope with the power, lightened body panels and modified nose, they were MkIIAs. The model had undergone a successful 24-hour trial at Ford's Kingman, Arizona, test track and the 7.0 litre V8 had lasted a 48-hour dyno run. Power output was now in the region of 470–480 b.h.p. and the cars weighed around 1225kgs.

Ferrari, by contrast, was having a difficult time coping with a wave of strikes that was disrupting Italian industrial life. A refashioned P2, the P3, had been developed to counter the MkII menace but hadn't been sent to Daytona and only one example had been mustered for the subsequent World Championship events, in contrast to the usual expansive campaign. Two examples were rustled up for the French classic, while another was lent to NART.

The P3 was lower and wider than the P2, with wider track and wider wheels. The car was also lighter, and for Le Mans sported sleek, fully enclosed bodywork. Its engine benefited from high compression heads and was fuel injected to produce a healthy 420 b.h.p., while the transmission was re-designed around a conventional ZF gearbox. It added up to a thoroughbred package that had proved capable of leading the Sebring race.

Start of a major Ford-Ferrari conflict: the 1966 Le Mans race. Car No. 2 is the eventual winner, the Ford of McLaren/Amon. Photo: LAT.

Sadly, Maranello's Le Mans challenge was weakened during practice when star driver Surtees fell out with Team Manager Dragoni and quit the camp. That left works cars in the hands of Scarfiotti/Parkes and Bandini/Guichet. Although these pairings were able to keep the Ford armada in sight, they were hard pushed to do so. An official one-two classification for Ferrari after eight hours' racing flattered to deceive. Soon after midnight Scarfiotti became a victim of a multiple pile-up and although the second works car lasted almost twice as long before succumbing to transmission failure, it had not looked like upsetting Ford in the long run.

Not that Ford enjoyed good reliability. Of the eight MkIIs, only three saw the finish. Those three finished together in a mighty impressive demonstration, but the company's attempt to stage a dead-heat between McLaren/Amon and Hulme/Miles was foiled as McLaren outfumbled Miles to promote his own name, that of a growing sports-racing constructor in his own right. It was appropriate that Henry Ford should have started the race and appropriate, too, that two of the three MkIIs which hadn't succumbed to engine failure had (by a whisker) become the first cars ever to exceed 3,000 miles at Le Mans. The big corporation's sledgehammer was of commendable design.

Ferrari's back-up runners, outpaced by the leaders, showed no more stamina than the works P3s. NART's P3 failed, so did a modified P2 from the same stable. And for three customer P2/3s (the P3 chassis with the 4.4 litre s.o.h.c. engine) survival wasn't the order of the day, either. Nor was it for the Ford and Ferrari runners contesting the new 'Sports Car' class.

This 50-off homologated sports-racing class was the new home for the GT40 and at last gave a purpose in life to the 275LM. It saw five GT40s oppose three 275LMs and not one escaped unscathed. Thus, of the 20 Ford and Ferrari one-off and homologated prototypes that started the race, only three finished . . .

Four other big capacity prototypes took the start, of which the most interesting was a converted American Can-Am car supported (discreetly) by General Motors. This was the Chaparral, powered by 425 b.h.p. 5.4 litre Chevrolet 'stock block' V8. Developed by Texan driver/engineer

Ferrari ran strongly in 1966, but Ford had become too strong for it, the American giant at last using its vast resources to full effect. The Ferrari P3 was a refined, thoroughbred machine but was beaten from the outset. Photo: LAT.

Splashing en route to a memorable 1–2 for Ford; the Mk11 of McLaren/Amon (car No. 2) came home to beat the similar car of Miles/Hulme (No. 1) by the narrowest of margins. Photo: LAT.

Jim Hall with the financial support of fellow driver 'Hap' Sharp, the '65 US Road Racing Championship winning machine featured a g.r.p. monocoque, an advanced appreciation of aerodynamics (in particular, the role of downforce) and a GM-developed, clutchless transmission. It made its European debut in the 'Ring 1000kms, which it won. Not surprisingly, it was overshadowed by the bigger displacement Fords at Le Mans, and not surprisingly it failed to last its Le Mans debut, retiring Saturday evening with electrical problems. But Chaparral would be back, strengthened. The three other interlopers in the big prototype battle were less credible efforts: two Bizzarinis and one Serenissima. All from Italy, all slow and fragile.

Behind the Ford/Ferrari wars was a 2.0 litre struggle between Ferrari and Porsche, and again Ferrari lost. Indeed, after only 100 minutes Porsche had seen the last of the Ferrari 'Dino'. Stuttgart's 2.0 litre prototype Carrera 6 models ran home first, second and third in class, then first in homologated 2.0 litre cars, filling fourth to seventh places overall. The team only lost one car, a second homologated Carrera (these without the benefit of long tails) which broke a con rod in the final hour. Porsche had speed *and* reliability.

Eighth overall was a rare Ferrari survivor, a 275 GTB which won the new GT class for 500-off models. It overcame a spate of broken wheels and a Porsche 911 (reliable, of course).

After the event Ford did not, as anticipated, pull out of prototype racing. However, it did wind up its FAV operation. Wyer later revealed that at this stage it was discovered that parts he had requested to make the 4.7 GT40 reliable were found to be in existence. He suggests they had been deliberately held back until such time as the MkII had won. Corporation man will play fanatical political games! But at the end of the day the big corporation has the power to get him what he wants. And enough of Ford's corporation men wanted more...

1.	7.0 Ford* (McLaren/Amon)	6.	2.0 Porsche (de Klerk/Schutz)
2.	7.0 Ford (Miles/Hulme)		* Class winners. Also:
3.	7.0 Ford (Bucknum/Hutcheson)	7.	2.0 Porsche (Klass/Stommelen)
4.	2.0 Porsche* (Siffert/Davis)	8.	3.3 Ferrari (Courage/Pike)
5.	2.0 Porsche (Herrmann/Linge)	9.	1.3 Alpine-Renault (Grandsire/Cella)
		14.	2.0 Porsche (Dewes/Kerguen)

1967

Stung by defeat, Ferrari produced more sophisticated cars with three valves/cylinder fuel-injected heads based on Forghieri's Grand Prix motors. But again Maranello was defeated by the sheer size of Detroit muscle.

This year both Ford and General Motors were playing the big capacity game and the alloy, four carburettor-fed 7.0 litre V8 wheeled out by Chevrolet was certainly a match for the familiar elephant engine it challenged.

Both pushrod motors fell a long way short of the 125 b.h.p. per litre achieved by the 36-valve Ferrari V12 but, with the best part of a 100 b.h.p. advantage, that wasn't of great concern. Great dollops of torque were more significant. If Ferrari had pedigree and engine sophistication, Ford and Chaparral-Chevrolet had brute power and awesome speed. And when it came to chassis sophistication, the Chaparral topped the lot. The g.r.p. monocoque device featured a new body profile calculated to produce higher downforce without a significant drag penalty. That performance was aided by an adjustable high rear wing, mounted directly on the uprights. It was activated by foot pedal: flat for maximum speed on the straight, tilted forwards for maximum downforce (and a braking effect) under cornering.

Very effective Hall's 2F proved. With a 250kg weight advantage it was a match for Ford's latest offering, the advanced monocoque construction MkIV, but it had one flaw: its V8's torque was unkind to its clutchless transmission.

Like the Chaparral, the new Ford was designed and built in the USA. It was a development of Roy Lunn's so-called 'J-car', seen in practice at Le Mans in '66 and featured a glued aluminium honeycomb monocoque tub, plus a new, narrow cockpit body shape for better wind penetration. Lunn had pushed for a new, lighter, lower drag chassis to accept the 7.0 litre Ford V8 in the wake of the '65 disaster – the original GT40 chassis was perceived as too heavy, a problem affecting acceleration, braking, fuel economy and reliability. The J-car alternative had been approved in October '65 and the new honeycomb monocoque (saving around 50kgs) had been promptly constructed by a company specializing in aircraft honeycomb structures. Although a runner by April '66, the car initially proved slower than the MKII in a straight line. Development was not hurried. A Can Am version had been played with in late '66, only for Miles to lose his life testing it.

An awesome line of big capacity prototypes for the 1967 Le Mans race with Ford MkIV and Chaparral monsters in the top three starting positions. Quicker off the mark is the Ford Mk11 of Bucknum/Hawkins which will star in the opening laps. Photo: LAT.

The J-car had been taken to Daytona early in '67, only for the MkII, again, to prove faster. However, all the MkIIs in this year's 24-hour Florida race broke. Again, excessive weight took the blame. Lunn was given a green light to develop the J-car for Le Mans...

Rebodied as the MkIV, the honeycomb Ford proved faster than the MkII in a straight line and won the Sebring 12 Hours. At Le Mans it was worth a 50kgs weight saving, according to the ACO scales, and an extra 7 m.p.h. of Mulsanne speed, reaching an all-time high of 213.1 m.p.h. The back-up MkIIs were in 'B' trim with similar heavier iron block engine rated at 500 b.h.p., a roll cage for extra driver protection, and various small modifications.

In spite of Ford's improvements, the company was hard pushed to knock the faster of Hall's two Chaparrals off pole. There were four MkIVs on hand, two each from Shelby and Holman Moody, but only the Shelby car of McLaren/Donohue went faster than the Hill/Spence Chaparral.

Come the race, the flightless American bird made a poor start. However, the MkIVs were also, surprisingly, beaten away by Shelby's back-up MkIIB, driven by Bucknum. The Bucknum/Hawkins MkII led for over an hour, then a water pipe split, leaving the MkIVs in the limelight. In front were the Gurney/Foyt Shelby MkIV, pressurized by the McLaren/Donohue sister car and the Holman Moody MkIV of Andretti/Bianchi. The Chaparral was right in there, too. Holman Moody's second MkIV had already been delayed by a sticking throttle and at around 10.00 p.m. the team suffered another setback when a gear linkage problem delayed Andretti/Bianchi. Shortly afterwards Ruby parked the sister car, in which Hulme had set fastest lap, in a sand bank.

By midnight Shelby was feeling very comfortable, for the Chaparral's wing had stuck in the downforce position, knocking off 30 m.p.h. on the Mulsanne. The Gurney/Foyt car was now one lap ahead of the McLaren/Donohue machine, while Andretti/Bianchi were looking for a way back to third, past the highest-placed Ferrari P4. Alas, just before half distance Holman Moody lost all hope: Andretti crashed out with brakes locked.

When McLaren/Donohue suffered a clutch malady, and with the MkIIBs sidelined, the way was open for Ferrari's three surviving (of four) P4s to hold second, third and fourth positions, albeit half-a-dozen laps behind the troublefree MkIV. Shelby's hopes of recovering a one-two

The Ferrari P4 was a classic racing car with its three valves/cylinder V12 engine and attractive, slippery shape. Alas, in 1967 sophistication alone was not sufficient... Photo: LAT.

situation were dashed by lost bodywork for the clutch-delayed car, while Chaparral's hopes of a finish were dashed by transmission trouble (the slower car having succumbed early to electrical problems).

Although unable to keep pace with the fastest Detroit monsters, at the end of the day Ferrari was only beaten by one of the beasts. It was a great achievement for the Italian team to bring home two cars in good shape, given the fact that its cars had to be flogged mercilessly to stay in contention. Both survivors broke the distance record, achieving over 5000kms, to leave the delayed McLaren/Donohue car in fourth place. The Ferrari failures were the P4 of Amon/Vaccarella (fire when fuel line was sheared by running on a flat) and Klass/Sutcliffe (sheared injection pump). The car which finished second was in the hands of Parkes/Scarfiotti and was driven extremely hard throughout, reducing the leaders' deficit on Sunday, if four laps adrift at the finish. It had lost with honour.

Behind the second-placed P4 was a loaned example in the colours of the ENB, driven by Mairesse/Beurlys, this the only P4 let out of captivity. Whereas the P4 had a revised fuel-injected engine, wider track and subtle chassis modifications, other customer teams had to be content with a so-called 'P3/4', a combination of P3 24-valve, carburettor engine and P4 shell. All three such entries retired due to engine failure, while the oldest of Ferrari's eight-strong prototype fleet, NART's P2, had been its first drop-out, stuck in a sand bank.

Ford's back-up prototypes had been no more fortunate – the Bucknum/Hawkins car had eventually retired with engine failure, while

Brute force and chassis sophistication was the winning formula for Ford in 1967. This is the big pushrod V8 equipped MkIV of winners Gurney and Foyt. Photo: LAT.

From Texas came a new appreciation of the role of aerodynamic downforce in race car performance. This is the 1967 Chaparral which introduced the wing to Le Mans competition. Photo: LAT.

two other MkIIBs, both Holman Moody-prepared, had been eliminated in the wake of the Andretti accident.

Overshadowed by the American and Italian prototypes were four entries from the UK. The Slough-based FAV operation had been taken over by John Wyer and partner John Willment, who formed J. W. Automotive (JWA). With backing from Gulf, this new team entered two modified GT40s – lightened and re-profiled, they were known as Mirages. They were equipped with enlarged, 5.0 litre engines which gave trouble early in the race. The two other British-based machines were by that stage already in the pits suffering engine maladies. These were 5.0 litre Aston Martin V8-engined Lola T70s, cars run on behalf of Aston Martin and Broadley's Lola concern by John Surtees. Alas, while Broadley's latest monocoque chassis was workmanlike and well sorted, the new d.o.h.c., two-valve fuel-injected alloy engine was not yet race ready. Its embarrassingly early demise marked the end of an all-too-brief Aston Martin come-back.

With only four of the 21 big banger cars at the finish and all three GT40s which comprised the over 2.0 litre 'Sports Car' entry by the wayside, the way was left clear for Porsche's 2.0 litre runners to complete the top six once more. Shrugging off a threat from Matra (the French aerospace concern which was developing a State-supported Formula One engine behind the scenes) it brought four of six cars home, winning both 2.0 litre prototype and 'Sports Car' classes. Both Matra and Porsche had designs on new 3.0 litre engines and there were moves afoot which would put those engines in a very significant new context...

1.	7.0 Ford*	* Class winners. Also:
	(Gurney/Foyt)	7. 2.0 Porsche
2.	4.0 Ferrari*	(Elford/Pon)
	(Scarfiotti/Parkes)	9. 1.3 Alpine-Renault
3.	4.0 Ferrari	(Grandsire/Rosinski)
	(Beurlys/Mairesse)	11. 3.3 Ferrari
4.	7.0 Ford	(Steinemann/Spoerry)
	(McLaren/Donohue)	13. 1.5 Alpine-Renault
5.	2.0 Porsche*	(Vinatier/Bianchi)
	(Siffert/Herrmann)	16. 1.3 Abarth
6.	2.0 Porsche	(Martin/Mesange)
	(Stommelen/Neerpasch)	

1968

An era had passed. The monsters were gone. It wasn't so much a case of Detroit retiring its muscle cars from active service (although, for its part, Ford had little left to prove), more a case of them being shut out. Along with the rival Maranello machines. Powerful cars were no longer welcome at Le Mans. The largest capacity prototype displaced 3.0 litres.

Behind the new capacity limit for World Championship races had been growing concern at the speeds being reached by the big bangers, particularly at La Sarthe. The decision had been a knee-jerk one, taken immediately after the 1967 24-hour race. Or had it? There were those who stood to gain by it and few losers, as Ford was expected to retire in any case...

The decision had been to implement a 3.0 litre limit *as from the start of the following season*. That gave manufacturers precious little time in which to prepare... Ferrari withdrew, better to concentrate upon Formula One. The North Americans had no cause to turn to 'pony car' engines. However, the Ford badge would continue to be worn on the 'Sports Car' class GT40, 50-off homologated machines being allowed 5.0 rather than 3.0 litres, although having to run at 800 rather than 650kgs minimum weight. Homologated for the new season were the GT40, the Lola T70 with 5.0 litre Chevrolet V8 and the elderly Ferrari 275LM.

Foremost among the GT40 runners was JWA, which had resolved to revert to the overweight '65 design until such time as it could prepare its own 3.0 litre prototype. Running as a homologated car ruled out the 'Mirage' modifications seen in '67, but advantage was taken of the homologation of a full 5.0 litre version of the regular V8, with improved Gurney-Weslake heads. The JWA cars also had carbon fibre reinforced g.r.p. substitute body panels in the interests of weight saving. The highly competent British team, with solid Gulf backing, was one of only two serious contenders for the 1968 World Championship. The other was Porsche.

Encouraged by the performance of its 2.0 litre prototypes, the Stuttgart marque had commenced work on a 3.0 litre successor even before the 3.0 litre ceiling had been announced. It hadn't expected to beat the big bangers at fast circuits, but knew that with its expertise at ultra-light chassis construction it could be a challenger for outright honours elsewhere. Of course, the 3.0 litre ruling put its programme in new perspective. After 15 years of small capacity class competition it was suddenly taking on all-comers at all circuits.

104

The 2.0 litre Porsche 907 that had run so successfully at Le Mans in '67 hadn't been of a particularly sophisticated design. It had featured a straightforward spaceframe chassis and simple, air cooled flat six engine derived from the marque's 911 road car. For '68 that was to be superseded by an air cooled flat eight of similar general conception, with magnesium crankcase, aluminium blocks and two valve twin cam heads, displacing 3.0 litres and producing 335 b.h.p. (112 per litre), which was fed through a new six-speed gearbox.

The bigger engine wasn't ready for early season races but a 2.2 litre 907 won two of the first three events. And when the 908 arrived, it wasn't reliable. As the season progressed, the light (670kg) 908 was a match for the GT40's speed but lacked staying power, largely because of an engine vibration problem. Le Mans was postponed until September due to French domestic upheavals, yet still Porsche knew that its four-strong 908 fleet was unlikely to last.

In the light of Porsche's uncharacteristic '68 reliability record, JWA's three-car GT40 team had to start as favourite. Sure enough, the 908s led the opening phase only to fall by the wayside – to the extent that after only four hours the carefully conducted Rodriguez/Bianchi GT40 was handed a lead it would be able to nurse, without a challenge from outside its own team, to the flag.

The third string JWA car in the hands of Miur/Oliver had been more spiritedly driven in the opening stages, only to end up in a sand bank, but the Hobb/Hawkins example was holding station in second place. However, after five hours it ran into a clutch problem which took the best part of two hours to fix. And then the engine blew anyway. The less competitive 'Sports Car' runners, two other GT40s, two Lola T70s and four Ferrari 275LMs, were no more successful – only one of them finished, a Ferrari in seventh place.

The big bangers are gone: the 5.0 litre J. W. Automotive GT40s (cars 10 and 11) were the biggest capacity prototypes in '68 and were handicapped by a weight penalty compared to 3.0 litre rivals, such as Alpine Renault (car No. 29). Photo: LAT.

The equally fragile if slippery long tail 908s (which, just shy of 200 m.p.h. on the Mulsanne, had headed practice) had been badly afflicted by alternator failures. The first such breakage had occurred after only three hours, but already the fastest of the four (Siffert/Herrmann) had been sidelined by a broken gearbox casing. The alternator problem took care of two cars and cost the third an hour in the pits. Nevertheless, driven by Stommelen/Neerpasch, that one at least finished in a flattering third place.

Splitting the winning GT40 and the troubled Porsche was one of three privately-entered 2.2 litre 907s which had been prepared at the factory as carefully as the works cars... Two had failed nevertheless (defective starter motor and engine failure), but Steinemann/Spoerry had done what the factory had expected of them, lapping consistently and profiting from the misfortunes of others...

It was a race in which most found misfortune. Unlucky was a four-car team of Alpine-Renault A220 3.0 litre prototypes and a lone works 3.0 litre Matra 620 prototype. Up from the 2.0 litre ranks (Alpine Renault with a Gordini-badged V8, Matra with its State-funded V12), the new French contenders for the outright win had been some way short of realistic victors. The Matra had been far more competitive than the Alpines but found itself having to look for second behind the old GT40. With that seemingly in the bag, a tyre had disintegrated and damaged its electrical system. Alpine managed one survivor, which struggled home behind the old Ferrari 275LM...

Alfa Romeo had managed to challenge the Matra with its *2.0* litre prototype. It had entered a four-car team of *Tipo* 33s and three finished, in fourth, fifth and sixth positions, damaged suspension having cost the fourth-placed car of Galli/Giunti a realistic hope of second following the demise of the Matra.

Less distinguished prototype performances came from a 3.0 litre Chevron-Repco and a 2.0 litre Healey-Climax – neither featured or finished – and from a pair of interesting Howmet turbine cars. Using Continental gas turbine engines equated to 3.0 litres, neither American entry played a significant part in the proceedings. One crashed, the other fell too far behind due to a broken hub bearing and was disqualified.

Altogether, it hadn't been an inspiring 24-hour race, due to the weakness of the prototype entry and the lack of spectacle, but Porsche was hatching plans which would give 'monster cars' a new lease of life...

1.	5.0 Ford* (Rodriguez/Bianchi)	6.	2.0 Alfa Romeo (Biscaldi/Casoni)
2.	2.2 Porsche* (Steinemann/Spoerry)		* Class winners. Also:
3.	3.0 Porsche* (Stommelen/Neerpasch)	9.	1.5 Alpine-Renault (le Guellec/Serpaggi)
4.	2.0 Alfa Romeo* (Galli/Giunti)	12.	2.0 Porsche (Gaban/Vanderschriek)
5.	2.0 Alfa Romeo (Facetti/Dini)	14.	1.0 Alpine-Renault (Andruet/Nicolas)

1969

Porsche might have thrown away its big chance in 1968 but it was heavily committed not to make that mistake again. Following a season of uncharacteristic unreliability it had turned its 3.0 litre prototype into a regular winner and had wrapped up the World Championship, even before the race it wanted to win above all. Against Ferrari opposition, to boot, although it has to be admitted that the Italian marque's return was a low-key one, pitting one, sometimes two cars, against a six- or seven-strong Porsche fleet.

The new Ferrari 312P was an open, low windscreen 'spyder' using Formula One mechanicals for chassis and engine. Its four valves/cylinder, 60 degree V12 (an evolution from the P4 4.0 litre engine) pumped out 420 b.h.p. – no less than 140 per litre and more than enough to deal with the Porsche flat eight. However, Porsche countered with exotic weight-saving materials and careful streamlining. Ferrari, the equal of Porsche for speed but not stamina over the balance of the '69 season, replied with a coupé top for Le Mans, but on its reliability record its reinforced spaceframe prototype didn't look a 24-hour winner. Neither did the 3.0 litre challenge from Matra, less so that from Alpine Renault, neither marque on Porsche's pace. In June, 1969, the tide was running in Porsche's favour – and JWA couldn't hold much hope for its rugged but outpaced GT40s.

Even among the 'Sports Car' entry the GT40 looked outmoded: Porsche had a brand new homologated runner which weighed little more than the 800kg minimum, yet produced a formidable 585 b.h.p. The marque had taken advantage of the reduction of the homologation quantity from 50 to 25, producing a 25-off batch of 'super 908s' with 12 cylinders and therefore a 4.5 litre displacement. With two valves per cylinder and air cooling mitigating against a high b.h.p. per litre, Porsche had been at a disadvantage in the 3.0 litre race. At a stroke it was out in its own race for state-of-the-art 4.5 litre prototypes...

In fact, the remarkable 917 produced 12 b.h.p. per litre more than the 908 from which its engine was derived and, running the Mulsanne at over 200 m.p.h., pushed lap speeds up to the levels of the mid-Sixties. The opposition could but hope that the as yet unproven machine (it had only made its race debut the previous month) would lack staying power. It certainly lacked development, its handling on the limit very tricky. Although its chassis was derived from the spaceframe 908, the long block pushed the driver well forward. In fact, the engine was particularly long as

The remarkable Porsche 917 brought a new breed of lightweight five litre race engine equipped prototype to La Sarthe in 1969 and came close to winning the race. It was stopped only by its newness. Photo: LAT.

it had a centre-crank power take-off – it was not simply a flat 8 with four extra cylinders, although in many respects it followed the smaller engine's design.

Four 917s were on hand: two race cars plus a spare for the factory (backed up by four 908s), plus one for the first customer – English entrant/driver John Woolfe. Woolfe's co-driver was unimpressed by the 917's track behaviour and stood down, so the factory lent one of its test drivers for the race. He didn't get a turn – driving hard on the first lap, Woolfe crashed at Maison Blanche and was killed.

The incident eliminated the Amon/Schetty Ferrari and broke up the field, but in any case the works 917s were long gone – the cars of Elford/Attwood and Stommelen/Ahrens *almost* unchallengeable. The only car to be able to stay in touch was a unique long-tailed Porsche 908 spyder driven by Porsche star driver Siffert/Redman. Alas, its new shape didn't allow adequate transmission cooling and the gearbox broke after four hours.

The opposition prayed for the 917s to break. Stommelen/Ahrens started losing oil after six hours but Elford/Attwood continued to run strongly throughout the night. Stommelen/Ahrens retired with clutch failure. Only retirement stood between Elford/Attwood and the podium...

Surprisingly, the remaining coupé-bodied 908s weren't dominating the pursuing prototypes. First Herrmann/Larrousse had lost 20 minutes due to a wheelbearing failure, then Schutz had crashed a sister car into retirement. Mind you, Ferrari was also in difficulty, its second coupé afflicted by gearbox woes which proved terminal. It was Matra that had shown strongest in the chase overnight but on Sunday morning its lead car (Beltoise/Courage) needed a long stop to rectify a wiring problem. None of the other French 3.0 litre cars (Matra and Alpine Renault had four apiece this year) had featured, so the 917 was left four laps ahead of the steady Lins/Kauhsen 908 which in turn was four laps ahead of the steady pair of JWA GT40s as mid-morning approached. However, by this stage the 917's clutch was showing signs of imminent failure. First, Kauhsen/Lins's apparent windfall was dashed by differential failure...

The 917 finally crept in to surrender the lead to JWA at 11.00 a.m. Porsche had one last hope, the recovering Herrmann/Larousse coupé. At midday it unlapped itself. Just after 12.40 Larrousse handed to Herrmann for a 75-minute dash to the (early) finish. Oliver's leading GT40 set the German back a lap as he joined the fray but the Ford needed one more fuel stop. During this Oliver handed to Ickx, who found himself less than

The 3.0 litre Grand Prix engined Ferrari Spyder was fitted with fully enclosed bodywork for the 1969 Le Mans race but, fast elsewhere, in coupé form its speed was disappointing and its Formula One gearbox was its weakness. Photo: LAT.

a lap ahead. With half-an-hour to run he saw Herrmann's faster 908 on his tail. However, the Porsche's brake warning light was now glowing. Herrmann went ahead, only for Ickx to slip back in front under braking. The GT40 could use the faster car's slipstream on the Mulsanne, then dive ahead under braking to lead through to the completion of each lap. Thanks to Ickx's racecraft, he was ahead in the closest racing finish in Le Mans' history...

The winning GT40 was the same chassis that had taken the honour in 1968. Accompanied by its sister car, it had only slowly risen up the order. It could easily have finished second, for Hobbs/Hailwood had been in front when a brake caliper had cost seven minutes in the pits. Driving more conservatively at the end, their car came home less than 12 minutes in arrears to claim third place.

Behind the drama, Matra had plenty to be pleased about, even if its two quickest cars had both been afflicted by problems. It lost one car but the others came home fourth, fifth and seventh. In contrast, the Alpines all retired, their less powerful V8s bugged by breakages.

Splitting the Matra formation was another GT40 (Kelleners/Joest), a private entry that ran as steadily if not as fast as the JWA cars. In contrast, two Lola T70s typically suffered failed Chevrolet V8 engines, while a lone Ferrari 275LM again registered a result (eighth) for the old soldier. 1969 had been a good year for the old 'Sports Cars' but clearly the future lay with a new strain of this animal...

1.	5.0 Ford* (Ickx/Oliver)	6.	5.0 Ford (Kelleners/Joest)	
2.	3.0 Porsche* (Herrmann/Larrousse)		* Class winners. Also:	
		9.	2.0 Porsche (Poirot/Maublanc)	
3.	5.0 Ford (Hobbs/Hailwood)	10.	2.0 Porsche (Gaban/Deprez)	
4.	3.0 Matra (Beltoise/Courage)	12.	1.0 Alpine-Renault (Serpaggi/Ethuin)	
5.	3.0 Matra (Guichet/Vaccarella)			

1970

Two of the world's greatest sports car manufacturers locked in combat, each equipped with over half-a-dozen of the fastest, most powerful cars ever seen at La Sarthe: it had all the makings of a Hollywood epic. It was appropriate, then, that Steve McQueen's Solar Productions company should chose 1970 for the making of the film *Le Mans*.

This year the leading roles were played by the Porsche 917 and Ferrari's response to it, the 512. The 917 had been greatly improved by aerodynamic alterations suggested by JWA, which was now running the works team, while the 512 was a developing 5.0 litre, 25-off prototype built with the financial support of Fiat, which had taken Ferrari under its wing. The big, 900kg Ferrari coupé was propelled by a new, 570 b.h.p., four-valve V12 (again, based on the P4 engine), to which Porsche had responded with a flat 12 bored and stroked to 4.9 litres, officially rated at 600 b.h.p. (122 per litre).

Through early season races the dominant force had been JWA's 'factory' Porsche team using Slough-prepared chassis and Stuttgart-prepared engines. Porsche continued to carry out development work on

While J. W. Automotive ran the regular works 917 race programme in 1970, Porsche developed a long tail version of its highly successful model specifically for Le Mans. JWA declined the '917LH': this example driven by Elford and Ahrens was in effect a factory car racing against the factory's contracted team. Photo: LAT.

the car, and through its customer service department prepared two more entries for Porsche Salzburg. JWA refused a Porsche-developed long tail for Le Mans, instead relying on its own modification to the standard tail. The factory therefore equipped both the Salzburg and the private German Martini team with an example of its low drag, long tail 917 *Lang Heck*, which was faster on the Mulsanne but didn't handle so well.

JWA fielded three 917 *Kurz:* 4.9s for regular crews Siffert/Redman and Rodriguez/Kinnunen, plus a 4.5 litre back-up car, while Porsche Salzburg had the 4.9 917LH (Elford/Ahrens) plus a 4.5 917K (Herrmann/Attwood). With the Martini 4.5 917LH and a factory fettled 4.5 917K entered by Solar Productions, that was some seven-car line-up for the race that was to be flagged off by Ferry Porsche with, for the first time, the drivers sitting in their cars.

Elford showed the worth of the long tail in practice, clocking 227 m.p.h. en route to pole. However, in spite of a 14 m.p.h. speed disadvantage, the 30kg lighter, better handling JWA 917K in Siffert's hands was only one second slower over a complete lap. Splitting the two fastest Porsches was the first of no less than eleven 512S models, four of which were long-tail works cars driven by Vaccarella/Giunti, Ickx/Schetty, Merzario/Regazzoni and Bell/Peterson.

Although heavier than the 917LH, the as yet less well developed 512S was a good match on all-round performance. However, Maranello's practice pace was not backed up by such impressive race form. Fast man Vaccarella lasted less than an hour before a con rod fractured. By the one-hour mark it was raining hard and 917s held the top five positions (led by the 4.9 litre trio), chased by Ickx/Schetty.

The Rodriguez car was the first Porsche loss, suffering a broken con rod after one-and-a-half hours' running. However, through a rainy

Long tail Ferrari 512S chases long tail Porsche 917LH through the Ford chicane, with a couple of lesser machines in between making life busier for the fast men. The '70 Ferrari versus Porsche contest went strongly in Porsche's favour. Photo: LAT.

evening the other 4.9 litre Porsches ran away from the pack, JWA and Salzburg vying for the lead. Meanwhile, a multiple car pile-up claimed four more of the six fastest 512s, two of them works cars. The only remaining factory runner was the well-placed Ickx/Schetty machine.

After seven hours the rivalry within the Porsche ranks went off the boil, a deflating tyre leaving Siffert/Redman only Ickx/Schetty to worry about. However, that car soon hit a big puddle and crashed, tragically claiming the life of a marshal. Not long after, the leading British-based car was over-revved, Siffert missing a gear. The team's back-up entry had already been crashed on a wet track, as had the Solar Productions example. But Porsche still had a few fit runners. Inheriting the lead was the Herrmann/Attwood 917K, chased by the team's delayed stream-liner . . . which was still three laps behind when its engine cried enough at 8.30 a.m. Overnight the remnants of the Ferrari challenge had crumbled completely: along with the six fastest cars, two of which had been prepared by Scuderia Filipinetti, on the sidelines were three of the other private entries, two with broken gearboxes, the other with accident damage.

In spite of a misfire, Herrmann/Attwood ran home victors ahead of the Martini 917LH, which in turn was followed by the class-winning 3.0 litre prototype, the same team's ex-works 908/2 spyder. Ferrari had to be content with fourth and fifth places for its 512S survivors, the NART example on 11 cylinders, that of Ecurie Francorchamps delayed by fuel feed bothers.

If, due partly to the rain, the big car entry had rather fallen apart, the prototype reliability score was even worse. Favourites had been three Matras, flying the Tricolour alone as Renault had pulled the unsuccessful Alpines out of racing. The Matras enjoyed improved V12 engines but had lost reliability. Alfa Romeo had moved up to 3.0 litres and fielded a four-car team of V8 *Tipo* 33s but had been no more successful. Of the four other prototype runners (two ex-works 908/2s, one ex-works Ferrari 312P and a works Healey) only the aforementioned Lins/Marko Martini entry had made the classification. Particularly unlucky had been the Healey, now running with 3.0 litre Repco engine. After two slight accidents, starter troubles and a gearbox rebuild, it looked set for a finish, if nothing else, when with 15 minutes to run the ignition died.

In 1970 the one-off prototypes had been overshadowed as surely as the only survivor of the 'sports car' old guard, a Lola T70-Chevrolet which lasted nine hours. Wet or dry, the race belonged to 25-off prototypes with Porsche, so long the champion of the little car, to the fore . . .

1.	4.5 Porsche* (Herrmann/Attwood)	5. 5.0 Ferrari (de Fierlant/Walker)
2.	4.5 Porsche (Larrousse/Kauhsen)	6. 2.0 Porsche* (Chasseuil/Ballot-Lena)
3.	3.0 Porsche* (Marko/Lins)	* Class winners. Also:
4.	5.0 Ferrari (Bucknum/Posey)	7. 2.3 Porsche (Kremer/Koob)

1971

For Porsche, 1970 had been a very satisfactory season, culminating as it did in a highly-prized and overdue Le Mans win. New partner JWA had enjoyed much success but had not achieved the anticipated Le Mans hat-trick and had been dismayed to have found itself racing what amounted to a second factory-supported team in addition to rival marques. Porsche registered its dissatisfaction and at the end of the season the Salzburg team was disbanded; only to be replaced by Hans Dieter Dechent's Martini team. For its part, the factory had found JWA's conservative (if successful) approach sometimes frustrating and had resorted to trying out development tweeks on the second team's 'customer' cars. With Ferrari concentrating upon a 3.0 litre prototype in '71 (in anticipation of the expulsion of the 5.0 litre cars from the end of the season) the battle of the year was JWA versus Martini, although Ferrari's swiftest customers were not to be discounted.

Ferrari had designed its new prototype specifically as a lightweight 1000km machine and left its 24-hour representation to its 512 customers, after putting a cat among Porsche's quasi-works pigeons on a number of occasions. Sadly, Alfa Romeo was also absent. Its latest 3.0 litre runner, although not as swift as the Ferrari 312P, had run regularly and reliably enough to profit from Porsche problems in winning three World Championship races.

Apart from those dents to its pride, Porsche had continued to dominate the World Championship leader board, JWA once again delivering the goods on a regular basis. The factory had developed a full 5.0 litre engine offering 10% more torque and for Le Mans had a more satisfactory long tail, which JWA was happy to exploit. Once again the British squad fielded three cars, including a one-off back-up machine (in short tail trim) and Martini matched this with one streamliner, one short car and an experimental factory device, an ugly, dumpy machine painted to represent cuts of pork and therefore known as 'The Pig'. Apparently, unknown to JWA and even its own drivers, the short tail Martini car had a new magnesium spaceframe.

In the face of six front line Porsches, Ferrari's great white hope was a 512M – the lighter, more aerodynamic version of the 512S which had shaken the 917 establishment when run by the works at the end of 1970 – entered by NART but run by the crack American Roger Penske team. The Penske 512M sported modifications by the team's renowned driver/engineer Mark Donohue and relied on a Traco-prepared V12. This season

J. W. Automotive found the Porsche factory's 1971 long tail of far more satisfactory design than the previous year's offering and agreed to race it. Alas, neither of the dominant Gulf-backed team's two 917 Langhecks *saw the finish. Photo: LAT.*

both Porsche and Ferrari had around 610 b.h.p. on tap. NART itself prepared two 512Ms, while others came from the leading European customer team Filipinetti – two cars, one a radically modified '512F' – owner/driver Jose Juncadella, Hughes de Fierlant, Georg Loos and David Piper. Nine in all, to face seven 917s, including a private car from Zitro Racing.

The smart money was on JWA and Rodriguez duly wrapped up pole with an average speed just a whisker over the 250 k.p.h. hurdle, while Elford's Martini streamliner pipped Siffert's similar car to the front row of the rolling start behind a Porsche pace car. Donohue and Vaccarella for Juncadella were breathing down Siffert's neck, and these five made the early running, along with the other JWA and Martini cars. For hour after hour the pace was that of a Grand Prix. After the first three hours the first six cars were still on the same lap in the order Rodriguez/Oliver, Elford/Larrousse, Donohue/Hobbs, Siffert/Bell, Marko/Van Lennep (in the magnesium car) and Vaccarella/Juncadella. An hour later found the game American Ferrari in second place, then its Traco V12 cried enough . . .

An American-engined Lola T70, the odd man out in the 'Sports Car' class, was another early retirement but the failure of its Chevrolet was far less significant, and easier to accept . . .

Not long after the demise of the fastest Ferrari, the Martini streamliner lost its fan and cooked its engine. That left JWA holding down first to third places, chased by the Juncadella 512M. Surprisingly, the only strong showing 3.0 litre car, Matra's lone entry, was now up to sixth, splitting the Martini team survivors.

At 11 p.m., Siffert/Bell required a new rear hub carrier, at the cost of 28 laps, then at around 3.00 a.m. both sister cars hit trouble – at mid-distance the fast Spanish Ferrari led. Rodriguez/Oliver had suffered the same hub carrier failure, probably due to overheating caused by the long tail bodywork, which fared in the rear wheels. It was repaired only for an oil line to burst, wrecking the engine. Meanwhile, Attwood/Muller's JWA 917K was losing time to a gearbox problem.

The Ferrari flags were out for only two hours of glory. Gearbox failure dashed Maranello's hopes. None of the remaining 512s were featuring. The magnesium 917K was left five laps ahead of the Amon/Beltoise Matra. The Pig had crashed.

The plucky 3.0 litre performance lasted until just before 9.00 a.m., by which time the Matra had been overhauled by the recovering JWA back-up car. Attwood/Muller had been instructed to make a win-or-bust effort, and with one hour to go had reduced the deficit to two laps. However, the Martini team had plenty in reserve . . . once again 'the other' factory team basked in glory.

Behind the two surviving 917Ks there was no sign of the delayed JWA streamliner. It had eventually succumbed to gearbox failure. However, there were two survivors of the Ferrari fleet, cars from NART and Piper, neither of which had avoided delay. Following the demise of the Matra, the 3.0 litre prototype class had fallen into the hands of an ageing 2.0 litre Porsche 907. None of the full 3.0 litre cars (four ex-works 908/2s, and a new Ligier GT prototype with Cosworth engine) was a finisher. However, next year the spotlight would again be on the one-off cars. With Matra's impressive pace, could a French revival be on the cards?

1.	4.9 Porsche* (Marko/van Lennep)	5.	4.4 Ferrari* (Grossmann/Chinetti Jnr)
2.	4.9 Porsche (Muller/Attwood)	6.	2.4 Porsche* (Touroul/Anselme)
3.	5.0 Ferrari (Posey/Adamowicz)		* Class winners. Also:
4.	5.0 Ferrari (Craft/Weir)	7.	2.0 Porsche (Brun/Mattli)

116

1972

A blanket 3.0 litre limit was what Ferrari, Alfa Romeo and Matra had been waiting for, but it did not suit Porsche. The World Championship had become an arena for Formula One-engined cars and its two-valve, air-cooled flat six didn't have sufficient muscle. Porsche opted to develop the 917 as a turbocharged Can Am car. Its withdrawal left the World Championship the preserve of Ferrari. Matra put all effort into Le Mans and the Maranello three-car team had no trouble in flattening the Alfa Romeo and Cosworth Ford-powered Lola and Mirage opposition, winning all eight races prior to Le Mans.

Faster than the outclassed Alfa Romeo, the Matra V12 prototype had only come up against the Ferrari V12 prototype at the Le Mans test weekend. The Prancing Horse was a whisker quicker. However, Matra could prepare for Le Mans in a confident frame of mind, following successful 24-hour tests at the Paul Ricard circuit in Southern France. Ferrari ran its own 24-hour test at Monza just three weeks before Le Mans and after 17 hours the clutch broke. The World Champion marque withdrew its entry.

Ferrari's withdrawal meant that after four years of trying, Matra simply had to win. Anything less would be sheer humiliation. The team entered four cars with different permutations of body design, engine specification, tyres and gearbox, in an attempt to ensure it had the right car, whatever the conditions. And with prize money to be equally divided, it was a real team effort.

The principle opposition consisted of three plodding Alfa Romeos, an under-financed, two-car, works-assisted Ecurie Bonnier Lola-Cosworth team, the latter relying on a drivetrain developed for two-hour Grands Prix. The speed of Bonnier's aerodynamic Lolas gave Matra a surprise in the early stages. At the end of the first lap the monocoque chassis French spyders came through one-two-three-five, a monocoque chassis Lola spyder hanging right in there. The next lap the partisan crowd expected one-two-three-four. Instead, one of the blue cars crawled past the grandstands and expired in a cloud of steam. Then, at the end of the third lap, Bonnier came through in the lead ...

Bonnier's glory didn't last long. The number one Lola was soon troubled by a gear selection problem. However, de Fierland's sister car took over the running and, as it started to rain, went even further ahead of the wailing V12 warriors. But the Lola went in for fuel ahead of the home runners and that was the end of the Cosworth challenge. Thereafter, Matra led throughout.

Cevert/Ganley and Hill/Pescarolo dominated the running while Jabouille/Hobbs overcame an early fuel feed problem which cost half-a-dozen laps, to regain third place by half distance. By 4.00 a.m., the Lola challenge was but a distant memory. De Fierlant had spun in the wet soon after dark, stalling his engine. He didn't manage to restart it but co-driver Larrousse did – only for the car to be disqualified for a change of driver away from the pits. The sister car had lost a lot of time to its gear selection problem and could but hope to recover a respectable position.

The Matra procession continued relentlessly, a French victory after all those years inevitable. Alas, the occasion was soured at 8.00 a.m. by a collision between Bonnier's Lola and a slower car which claimed the life of the popular entrant/driver.

Victory this sad Sunday was assured for Hill/Pescarolo when Ganley was hit by a slower car at the cost of nine laps. With minutes to go a one-two-three finish was still on the cards, only for the Jabouille/Hobbs car to break its gearbox...

In the wake of the first French victory since 1950, the Alfa Romeo team lost its chance of third place to a spate of transmission trouble. Having to hope for Matra to strike problems, it was the Italian team which had all its cars delayed – 6.30 a.m. found all in the pits having broken clutches replaced. Eventually, the Vaccarella/de Adamich entry came home fourth, behind the surprise of the race...

Matra's 3.0 litre V12 prototypes had been completely overshadowed during the era of 25-off 'sports cars' but in 1972 they were given the field to themselves through regulation changes and the absence of Ferrari. Photo: LAT.

Token opposition only for Matra in '72, in the form of Ecurie Bonnier's Lola-Cosworth spyders. Bonnier's own car claimed the lap record during a Matra dominated race, only for the entrant to lose his life on a black Sunday morning. Photo: LAT.

Porsche couldn't resist another involvement. Reinhold Joest was running an ex-works 908/3 in 1000km races and for the 24-hour marathon the factory offered him something more appropriate – a works-prepared 908 coupé. Although short of power, at 198.7 m.p.h. it was as fast as the blue cars on the Mulsanne and, tended by 'holidaying' factory engineers it ran like a Swiss watch...

Another consistent runner on the slightly revised circuit was the so-called Duckhams-Ford, a Cosworth-powered British monocoque special based on a Brabham Grand Prix car and built under the direction of driver Alain de Cadenet in a London mews garage. With Cosworth/Hewland drivetrain, it was carefully nursed to the finish but sadly an 'off' in the late, damp stages dropped it from fifth to 12th overall.

After the top four prototypes came the first of a vast number of GT cars. In '71 a lone Ferrari front-engined road car, the 365GTB 'Daytona' had finished fifth among the racers. This year seven Daytonas had come along to face seven Porsche 911s, four de Tomaso Panteras and four Chevrolet Corvettes. Only the 4.4 litre d.o.h.c. Ferrari V12 cars proved reliable, five of them filling the places from fifth to ninth overall. A splendid result for the marque which, Matra knew, might have a 24-hour prototype the following year...

1.	3.0 Matra* (Pescarolo/Hill)	6.	4.4 Ferrari (Posey/Adamowicz)
2.	3.0 Matra (Cevert/Ganley)		* Class winners. Also:
3.	3.0 Porsche (Joest/Weber/Casoni)	10.	2.9 Ford (Birrell/Bourgoignie)
4.	3.0 Alfa Romeo (Vaccarella/de Adamich)	13.	2.5 Porsche (Barth/Grant/Keyset)
5.	4.4 Ferrari* (Andruet/Ballot-Lena)	14.	1.8 Lola-Ford (Ligonnet/Smith)
		15.	7.0 Chevrolet (Heinz/Johnson)

1973

Having achieved its primary ambition in the sports car arena, Matra went on to tackle Ferrari on the 1973 World Championship trail – and had an edge. However, in spite of inferior pace, poor reliability for Matra kept Ferrari well up in the points race, which prompted it to tackle Le Mans. Both marques fielded long-tail versions of their regular spyder-bodied, Grand Prix V12-engined prototypes. Ferrari's semi-stressed engine, the 180 degree vee that was giving the Cosworth a good run for its money in Grand Prix racing, was now rated at 470 b.h.p. (157 per litre) in slightly detuned 1000km trim. Matra claimed an equal output for its fully stressed 60 degree vee. Both were, of course, four-valve, all-alloy units, the Ferrari with only four main bearings, the Matra with seven, and both were fed by fuel injection and electronic ignition systems. The French engine had suffered a number of worrying failures during the season but just prior to Le Mans designer Georges Martin traced these to insufficient lubrication of the small end and was able to effect a suitable cure.

Matra hadn't let its title bid compromise its Le Mans chances. Three brand new cars with rugged Porsche gearboxes were rolled out and in addition to these 'MS670Bs' for Beltoise/Cevert, Pescarolo/Larrousse and Jabouille/Jaussaud there was a regular Hewland gearbox MS670 for

Depailler/Wollek. Ferrari countered with plated-spaceframe 312PBs for Ickx/Redman, Merzario/Pace and Reutemann/Schenken. It showed its hand right at the start: Merzario/Pace played hare with gusto; Ickx/Redman played tortoise with equal commitment. After two hours the 'hare's' fuel collector pot burst, costing it six laps and putting the lead in the hands of Matra for the first time. The marque then held the top three positions, ahead of Schenken/Reutemann.

Matra's woes commenced after three-and-a-half hours – thrown treads cost Beltoise/Cevert eight laps, Jabouille/Jaussaud eleven. Then just before one-quarter distance the standard MS670's engine blew. Now three cars apiece, Ferrari was guarding first and second places, chased by Pescarolo/Larrousse.

At 2.30 a.m. Reutemann coasted out of the lead with a blown engine. It was Ickx/Redman versus Pescarolo/Larrousse and, as the Beltoise/Cevert car soon lost another tread and crashed into retirement, it came down to one delayed back-up car per marque. Merzario/Pace were holding a good margin over Jabouille/Jaussaud after each had encountered further problems.

Ferrari fortunes sank at breakfast time. The leading 312PB's exhaust fractured and the car sounded distinctly sick. When it fractured further with a risk of fire, it had to be replaced at the cost of a one-lap lead. However, no sooner had Matra taken over than it needed a rear brake hose. After both repairs the Matra emerged with a very slender advantage.

Ferrari might have won the 1972 World Championship but it had avoided confronting home hero Matra at Le Mans. 1973 saw the two giants of 'Seventies 3.0 litre prototype racing head-on at Le Mans and the French marque took another win . . . but only just. This Ickx/Redman Ferrari expired in the twenty-second hour when victory was still within grasp. Photo: LAT.

Ferrari took another blow at 11.00 a.m. when Ickx/Redman suffered the same split collector pot that had afflicted Merzario/Pace. Again the loss was six laps, so at midday the order was Matra, six laps, Ferrari, 10 laps, Ferrari, six laps, Matra.

Right on the stroke of 12, Pescarolo was making a routine stop. Two minutes later, his car wouldn't re-start. A rebuild of its starter got it away fractionally ahead of the Ferrari . . . which wasn't in such good health. The fractured exhaust had taken its toll and with two hours to run the flat 12 cried enough. To the delight of France, Pescarolo/Larrousse were able to cruise home six laps ahead of Merzario/Pace, while Jabouille/Jaussaud bagged third some 24 laps adrift.

The setbacks to the leading cars might well have opened the door for the Gulf Racing Research team, an offshoot from the disbanded JWA operation. This outfit ran Cosworth-powered 'Mirage' monocoque spyders with sturdy ZF gearboxes, which were well in the running from the word go. However, before two hours were up the Bell/Ganley M6 was in the pits with a serious lack of gears, which cost three hours. Nevertheless, the Hailwood/Schuppan car continued to run strongly and at midnight lay in an encouraging fourth position. Alas, that was as far as the team's challenge went – early Sunday brought a barrel roll accident for Schuppan.

The other Cosworth cars – two private Lolas plus the Duckhams – all fell by the wayside, while a privately run Alfa Romeo T33 TT V8, which performed creditably overnight, fell out of the reckoning due to a broken gearbox. The only other 3.0 litre prototypes were old Porsche 908s, two of which ran to top 10 positions.

This year the Porsche factory was officially represented in the prototype class – with a GT car. This was a heavily modified 911, the Carrera RSR, taking advantage of the freedom of the regulations to run many experimental modifications compared with the regular versions run in the 500-off GT class. Two entries were run and while one ran out of fuel the other took a solid fourth place. Less successful was a trio of Maserati-powered Ligiers, prototype GT cars entered on the same basis: the only survivor languished in 19th position.

The Carrera RSR in the GT class was beaten by Ferrari, the Daytona once again running out the winner, this year the best example taking a worthy sixth position. However, while the Italian concern clearly had a splendid GT workhorse for its privateers, its prototype team had slumped and internal politics were increasingly in favour of concentrating on Formula One. Sadly for sports car racing, the rot was about to set in.

1.	3.0 Matra* (Pescarolo/Larrousse)	5.	3.0 Porsche (Fernandez/Cheneviere/Torredemer)
2.	3.0 Ferrari (Merzario/Pace)	6.	4.4 Ferrari* (Elford/Ballot-Lena)
3.	3.0 Matra (Jabouille/Jaussaud)		* Class winners. Also:
4.	2.1t Porsche (Muller/van Lennep)	11.	3.3 BMW (Hezemans/Quester)
		12.	7.0 Chevrolet (Greder/Beaumont)

1974

Sadly, Ferrari's withdrawal signalled a serious decline in World Championship sports car racing. The big manufacturers were not lining up to race Grand Prix-engined prototypes. Grand Prix racing was being sustained by Cosworth-engined, British-built 'kit cars'. Alfa Romeo had produced an engine specifically for sports car racing but concentrated on 1000km events, which meant that only a handful of long-distance Cosworth kit cars stood between Matra and the hat trick.

Once again, the only real professional, well-funded prototype kit car was the Gulf Mirage – an uprated '73 model, the GR7. Revised and lightened, the team's two spyders were faster, but not fast enough to push Matra hard and, in any case, were struck by transmission trouble. One car retired Saturday night with a broken driveshaft, the other suffered dodgy c.v. joints and struggled home fourth.

The race belonged to Matra from the first lap to the last, always with the Pescarolo/Larrousse car in charge. By midnight it was out on its own – two sister cars had retired with broken engines, the third was overheating. It was nursed home to collect third place, so weak was the field.

Matra made it a hat trick in 1974, once again in the absence of Ferrari. This is the Pescarolo/Larrousse winning car. Photo: LAT.

The prototype casualty list included the Duckhams (suspension failure caused a dramatic spin into retirement in front of the pits), an old Lola, four older 908s and an even older ('69) 312P.

Once again Porsche and Ligier's GT specials ran as prototypes and once again the Porsche was a factor. This year it had equipped its RSR with a turbocharged 2.1 litre flat six (equated to 3.0 litres) – blown by a single KKK turbo it produced a healthy 450 b.h.p. One of the two turbo Porsches blew spectacularly on the Mulsanne overnight but the other ran trouble-free in the hands of Muller/van Lennep. When the leading Matra required an hour's surgery on Sunday morning it unwound its disadvantage, to arrive on the lead lap – but for a lost fifth gear it would have enjoyed the honour of leading. In any case, the Matra ran strongly once repaired, so a win was out of the question, though second place was very impressive.

In contrast, Porsche's regular GT RSRs had once more to take a back seat to the Daytona, examples of which took fifth and sixth positions, albeit only keeping the highest-placed 911 out of the top six by a whisker. So it was hat tricks for both Matra and Ferrari... amidst proposals that, with the impending withdrawal of the dominating prototype team, World Championship sports car racing should be restricted to prototype GT cars.

1.	3.0 Matra*	6.	4.5 Ferrari
	(Pescarolo/Larrousse)		(Heinz/Cudini)
2.	2.1t Porsche		* Class winners. Also:
	(Van Lennep/Muller)	15.	3.5 BMW
3.	3.0 Matra		(Aubriet/Depnic)
	(Jabouille/Migault)	17.	1.8 Chevron-Ford
4.	3.0 Mirage-Ford		(Beckers/Laurent/Fontaine)
	(Bell/Hailwood)	18.	7.0 Chevrolet
5.	4.5 Ferrari*		(Greder/Beaumont)
	(Grandet/Bardini)		

1975

The withdrawal of Matra and the sale of Alfa Romeo's prototypes to German enthusiast Willi Kauhsen left the World Championship bereft of factory prototype participation, save for Renault's Alpine competition wing, which ran a turbocharged 2.0 litre V6 car – that wasn't considered ready to face the rigours of Le Mans in its debut season.

The ACO introduced a fuel consumption limit in the form of a minimum number of laps between fuel stops and a maximum fuel tank size, which combined to call for a 25% m.p.g. improvement by 3.0 litre prototypes. The club thereby alienated itself from the struggling world series. But that had more serious long-term implications for the championship than for the prestigious French race...

Gulf Racing Research concentrated on the 24-hour classic, leaving the shorter races to Kauhsen and the new, experimental Alpine Renault. The

No Matra, no Ferrari. The Cosworth prototypes came into their own in 1975, detuned to meet new economy regulations. This is the Cosworth-propelled Schuppan/Jaussaud Gulf Mirage which finished third behind the winning sister car of Ickx/Bell and a Ligier-Cosworth. Photo: LAT.

strongest prototype team of 1975 had an improved GR8 design: still a Cosworth Ford-propelled spyder, detuned to around 370 b.h.p. in the interest of achieving the required 7.5 m.p.g. Its opposition consisted of two private Cosworth-propelled Lolas (one a new T380 spyder run by de Cadenet), four Porsche 908s (no longer at such a disadvantage in terms of power) and Ligier's GT prototype coupés. No longer facing Porsche factory opposition, the French concern had switched to Cosworth power for its two works cars, which were backed by a privately run Maserati version.

Not surprisingly, in the face of such weak opposition, the GR8s (Ickx/Bell and Schuppan/Jassaud) were fastest in practice and the design led all the way home. Ickx/Bell took over after the first pits stops and marched on to victory. The sister car lost its safe second place with an electrical failure on Saturday night, that cost half-an-hour. It had worked back into second by Sunday morning, only for rain to cause a further electrical failure. At the finish the two British cars were split by the only rival team that put any pressure on the Gulf effort: Ligier.

Although outpaced by the GR8 prototypes, the Lafosse/Chasseuil works JS2 ran steadily through the night and when the leading car suffered a broken exhaust on Sunday afternoon it moved onto the lead lap. It was a rousing performance by the home team, which had lost its other car to a series of mishaps – like the private car it had to be retired due to accident damage.

The de Cadenet Lola was the only other Cosworth Ford runner to finish, netting a lowly 15th place after shedding bodywork. The first three Cosworth cars were followed home by the survivor of the 908 fleet, an example run by Reinhold Joest and shared by its owner with Casoni and Barth. The next eight finishing positions were filled by GT Porsche Carreras, which this year dominated the overall entry, comprising over 50% of the race starters. In contrast just two Daytonas started, Ferrari development having lagged behind. The Italian GT car was only really useful at the French circuit, where its power could overcome its heavy front-engined-chassis handicap. Nevertheless, both V12 machines finished, just ahead of the unlucky de Cadenet.

It might have been an unlucky race for the British amateurs in that car, but it was a great weekend for the British professionals in the Gulf camp with the first British win since 1959. A shame that it was against so modest an opposition. Things could only get better...

1.	3.0 Mirage-Ford* (Ickx/Bell)	6.	3.0 Porsche (Faure/Cooper/Beurlys)	
2.	3.0 Ligier-Ford (Lafosse/Chasseuil)		* Class winners. Also:	
3.	3.0 Mirage-Ford (Schuppan/Jaussaud)	10.	3.0 Porsche (Maurer/Strahl/Beez)	
4.	3.0 Porsche (Joest/Casoni/Barth)	15.	2.1t Porsche (Beguin/Zbinden/Haldi)	
5.	3.0 Porsche* (Fitzpatrick/van Lennep)	21.	2.0 Moynet-Simca (Hoepfner/Mouton/Dacremont)	
		27.	2.0 BMW (Brillat/Gagliardi/Degoumois)	

1976

The struggling World Championship fragmented into two series, the World Sports Car Championship for conventional prototypes and the World Championship for Makes for GT-based machines. Neither was well supported. Le Mans opened its doors to protagonists of both, and to all comers. It was rewarded with the only bright entry of another bleak sports car season.

Porsche might have been committed to supporting new-style GT racing but as 1976 had approached it had become clear that only BMW would provide serious opposition. Worse, the alternative prototype series might well prove equally poor but a prototype would surely take the glory of Le Mans, even though the GT-based cars faced no capacity limit. The lighter weight and superior chassis ability of Alpine-Renault's 2.0 litre turbocharged prototype, with plenty of development behind it, looked a Le Mans-winning combination. Porsche resolved to produce its own turbocharged prototype.

Porsche's 936 spyder was essentially an evolution of its '72/73 917 Can Am chassis equipped with a further developed version of the flat six turbo seen in the '74 Carrera development car. With air/air intercoolers the power of the 2.142cc two-valve, air cooled engine was increased to 520 b.h.p. (243 per litre). The small, 911 road car-based unit was used as a semi-stressed member in the spaceframe chassis, which was hung with regular 917 running gear. A new bodyshape was devised to incorporate the latest ideas in aerodynamics, including a sizeable rear wing which was located at the end of the extended tail used at Le Mans. The car tipped the ACO's scales to 750kgs and reached 200 m.p.h. on the Mulsanne. However, in qualifying it didn't prove as swift as the Alpine-Renault it had beaten in opening rounds of the world series.

Alpine-Renault had responded to its '74 defeat by Kauhsen with an improved version of its 2.0 litre Renault-Gordini V6-engined turbo car. With similar aerodynamics to the 936, the A442 semi-monocoque Alpine-Renault's four-valve engine was rated at 500 b.h.p. and the car was just as

Porsche rejoined European prototype racing in 1976 with a 2.1 litre turbocharged machine. This example in the hands of Ickx and van Lennep took an easy win. Photo: LAT.

Alpine Renault produced a turbocharged 2.0 litre prototype to challenge Porsche in 1976 but the sole entry for Jabouille/Tambay/Dolhem, although fast enough to secure pole, never looked a likely winner and fell out overnight. Photo: LAT.

light as the Porsche.

The French team's sole entry didn't show its qualifying superiority in the race. Jabouille in the A442 and Ickx in the lead 936 had a good tussle in the opening laps, but even before Tambay had taken a turn at the wheel of the home runner it had been set back by an electrical fault and had developed worryingly high engine temperature. Porsche wasn't bothered by Alpine again. The French car recovered to take third place behind its two entries, only to expire at 1.30 on Sunday morning.

Half distance found Ickx/van Lennep two laps clear of Joest/Barth, both Porsche prototypes running sweetly and well in command of the proceedings. Only mechanical failure lay in the path of success and Joest/Barth were to experience it. At 7.10 a.m. their car rolled to a halt with a broken driveshaft only minutes after leaving the pits with an obvious engine malady.

Out on its own, the lead car had over 100 miles on its pursuers when the clock struck 12.00. Then a crack appeared in an exhaust pipe, running from the engine to the turbocharger. Twenty minutes were lost but the 936 had many more minutes to spare and cruised home 11 laps ahead of the Mirage of Lafosse/Migault.

Of the normally aspirated 3.0 litre prototypes running in the wake of the turbocars (two Mirage GR8s, two Lolas and two plodding Porsche 908s), the '75 winning design was favourite. The Gulf Racing Research project had been sold to wealthy American Harley Cluxton and at half distance his Cosworth-propelled spyders lay third (Lafosse/Migault) and fifth (Bell/Schuppan), the latter car delayed by a series of electrical failures. The de Cadenet Lola sat between them; the other, older Lola (surprisingly, the fastest Cosworth car in qualifying) had retired early. De Cadenet/Craft had been delayed by alternator problems and over the second half of the race put up a tremendous fight for the honour of finishing runner-up to the works Porsche team. The Lola came close to toppling Lafosse/Migault, while the second Mirage fell back to fifth, behind the leading GT runner, due to a failing engine.

Stuttgart's weapon for the new-look World Championship of Makes was a development of its 1974 Carrera with a larger, 2.9 litre engine reckoned to produce a healthy 590 b.h.p. The rival BMW CSL had a 3.2 litre four-valve engine reckoned to produce over 600 b.h.p. The end of the

128

1976 was to have been the year of the GT-based race car, but Le Mans was keen to retain prototypes to battle for outright honours, leaving 'Group 5' cars like this factory Porsche to strive for lesser honours. Stommelen/Schurti steered the Martini-backed runner to fourth place. Photo: LAT.

first lap saw the BMW ahead of the 935 Porsche and hard on the heels of the blown prototypes, but its moment of glory was only three laps long, then the under-developed car was in the pits with a serious oil leak.

Left at the head of the 'silhouette' GT cars, the Stommelen/Schurti works 935 was fast enough to have beaten the Cosworth prototypes home but was struck by all manner of problems, including a broken turbo. The red-hot component was changed in a cool ten minutes. The car went on to collect fourth place. The top six was rounded out by the winner of the homologated GT class, which this year was exclusively Porsche.

The ACO had also run classes for American IMSA GT cars and even American NASCAR stock cars, but none of the interesting US entries finished. Another innovation was the club's own 'GTP' category catering for coupé-bodied prototypes running to heavier minimum weights than the regular spyders and with engine regulations designed to attract a variety of solutions. The class attracted two new French teams, Rondeau and WM. Local man Jean Rondeau built and ran two Cosworth-powered semi-monocoque coupés under the name of sponsor Inaltera. WM (Peugeot stylist Gerard Weltier (W) and engineer Michel Meunier (M) prepared two coupés propelled by a 2.7 litre turbocharged Peugeot V6 – the same 'PRV' engine that formed the basis of the Renault Gordini V6.

Rondeau's was the more successful effort, overcoming many problems to get both cars home. Pescarolo/Beltoise took the GTP honours with an eighth place finish. That was something for France to celebrate, but the performance of Alpine-Renault suggested she might soon have an outright win to celebrate once more . . .

1.	2.1t Porsche*	* Class winners. Also:	
	(Ickx/van Lennep)	8.	3.0 Inaltera-Ford
2.	3.0 Mirage-Ford		(Pescarolo/Beltoise)
	(Lafosse/Migault)	12.	3.0t Porsche
3.	3.0 Lola-Ford		(Gadal/Segolen/Ouviere)
	(Craft/de Cadenet)	14.	3.0t Porsche
4.	2.8t Porsche*		(Laffeach/Miller/Vaugh)
	(Stommelen/Schurti)	15.	2.0 Lola-Ford
5.	3.0 Mirage-Ford		(Morand/Trisconi/Chavalley)
	(Bell/Schuppan)	24.	3.0 BMW
6.	3.0t Porsche*		(Ravenel/Detrin/Ravenel)
	(Cudini/Boubet/Touroul)		

1977

It had been hoped that by 1977 the World Championship for Makes would have been contested by many of Europe's leading performance car manufacturers. Instead, it had degenerated into a procession of Porsche 935s. Meanwhile, the alternative prototype series was the preserve of Alfa Romeo. Porsche and Alpine-Renault were conserving their '77 weapons for Le Mans...

The 24-hour classic was again the only bright spot. Its field lacked depth but still had variety and this year promised a bigger battle between Porsche and Alpine-Renault.

Following a surprising failure to win a single round of the Porsche-dominated '76 World Sports Car Championship, Renault's decision to concentrate on Le Mans brought a bigger entry from it; four cars. Like the two rival Porsches, these had been developed specifically for the 24-hour marathon. Porsche's concentration on the race went as far as narrowing the track of its prototype in the interests of higher Mulsanne speed. Both marques found more power as turbocharging technology developed. Porsche introduced twin turbos, one per cylinder bank, increasing output to 540 b.h.p., while Renault claimed 520 b.h.p. for its challenger.

Renault carried out extensive endurance testing at Paul Ricard and bolstered its chances by supplying engines to Cluxton's Mirage team, which once again ran two cars. Of the four works A442s, one was the test hack, entered privately but identical to the fresh factory cars.

Porsche's works 935 was its back-up. Development of its 2.9 litre twin turbo engine had yielded 650 b.h.p. and this endowed it with the fastest Mulsanne speed of all – 220 m.p.h. It was quick enough to act as Porsche's hare in the opening laps, hounding Jabouille in the pole position A442 before a loose rocker shaft cost three laps. Three hours later it retired with a blown engine.

Alpine Renault made a stronger, multi-car challenge in 1977 but once again was let down by poor reliability. This is the Laffite/Depailler A442. Photo: LAT.

Another victory for Porsche at Le Mans as Barth takes the sick car he was sharing with Ickx and Haywood across the line at 4.00pm on 12 June, 1977. Photo: LAT.

Renault similarly suffered a set-back in the first hour. In fact, on the very first lap. The privately-entered A442 caught fire as a result of a turbo oil line fracture.

The race settled down with Jabouille/Bell leading Ickx/Pescarolo, then the other Renaults of Depailler/Laffite and Tambay/Jaussaud, followed, at an increasing distance, by the Mirages. The second 936 was already out of contention, a fuel injection pump change costing over half an hour.

Just after the three-hour mark Porsche's position worsened – having been lapped by Jabouille, Pescarolo's 936 expired in a billow of smoke. A con rod had failed due to a manufacturing fault. Renault was fully in control of the situation. The surviving Stuttgart hope was in 41st position.

Ickx joined the crew of the delayed 936 and made it fly. Shattering the lap record, by 11.00 p.m. he had worked his way back through the pack, in front even of the Mirage-Renaults. Only the three surviving A442s lay ahead. Overnight the Jaussaud/Tambay example expired and the Depailler/Laffite car fell back due to a gearbox rebuild. Dawn revealed the leading car six laps ahead of the recovering 936. A comfortable advantage... but at 9.00 a.m. the Renault started trailing an ominous cloud of smoke. The team experienced its second piston failure. Ickx/Haywood/Barth were left two laps ahead of the surviving French car. Its piston failed at midday.

The leading 936 was out on its own – the Schuppan/Jarier Mirage was not fast enough with a '76 spec. engine, but was likely to go the distance. Its sister car had dropped out with nothing more serious than a dry fuel tank.

The hours drifted by... Suddenly, at 3.15 p.m. there was drama. The lead car slowed in a cloud of smoke and only just managed to struggle to its pit. Now Porsche had suffered a piston failure. But all was not lost. The turbos were isolated and the car was parked until 10 minutes from the finish. It was so far ahead that if it could complete two laps it would be classified as a finisher – in first place. Ickx having spent his maximum time at the wheel, Barth carefully coaxed the car the eight agonising miles to the flag...

131

1977 victors (from left) Ickx, Barth and Haywood. Their car had all but expired in the final hour but so weak was the opposition that it had been able to win as one of the walking wounded...

Still over 10 laps in arrears, in spite of the Porsche's wait, the Mirage duly collected second, but only after the demise of a quick Georg Loos-entered 935, which went the way of the team's sister car and a quick Kremer-entered example. However, the Ballot-Lena/Gregg 935 finished in third place and less than a minute ahead of an Inaltera crewed by Rondeau/Ragnotti.

This year the local team ran two lightened cars as 3.0 litre prototypes, in addition to a heavier GTP class version. Rondeau's lightweight was lucky to net fourth, being caught hand-over-fist by the similarly powered de Cadenet-Lola which, apart from an unmodified Lola, was the only other 3.0 litre prototype runner. Recovering from minor delays the de Cadenet-developed car (de Cadenet/Craft) fell only 92 seconds short of overhauling both third and fourth-placed cars.

The final car to pass the 300 lap mark was a 2.0 litre Chevron but the other Inalteras finished, winning GTP as the WM-Peugeots again fell by the wayside. GTP also contained a mish-mash of less competitive cars, including a heavily modified Aston Martin V8 Vantage saloon. Dealer Robin Hamilton brought the marque back to La Sarthe for the first time since 1967 and was rewarded with a trouble-free run to 15th place. The 1977 race had been nothing if not varied – but it had hardly been a memorable weekend for France. Renault badly wanted to concentrate on its challenging turbocharged Formula One programme, but first a matter of national as well as corporate pride was at stake...

1.	2.1t Porsche* (Ickx/Haywood/Barth)	5.	3.0 de Cadenet/Lola-Ford (de Cadenet/Craft)
2.	2.1t Mirage-Renault (Schuppan/Jarier)	6.	2.0 Chevron-ROC* (Pignard/Henry/Dufrene)
3.	2.9t Porsche* (Ballot-Lena/Gregg)		* Class winners. Also:
4.	3.0 Inaltera-Ford* (Rondeau/Ragnotti)	7.	3.0t Porsche (Wollek/Steve/Gudjian)
		8.	3.2 BMW (Xhenceval/Dini/Dieudonne)

1978

To check the growing Renault threat Porsche developed its first four-valve flat-six. Water cooled heads made the extra valves possible and 3.2 litre 935 and 2.1 litre 936 versions were produced simultaneously. The 1000kg silhouette GT's power plant was rated at 750 b.h.p. (234 per litre) and propelled a radical interpretation of the 935 chassis sporting long, flowing bodywork. Devoid of war paint, it resembled the Great White Whale. The prototype propulsion unit mustered something in the region of 550 b.h.p. (257 per litre) and, assisted by refined spyder aerodynamics, that was good enough for pole position.

But Renault hadn't been idle. It had tested cars at GM's Columbus, Ohio, proving ground, reckoning it needed a longer straight than Ricard could offer properly to prepare for the rigours of the Mulsanne. Overall, 10,000 miles' running had been clocked up and over 30 engine modifications had been instigated. Probably the most significant was greater piston thickness above the crankpin, allowed by a higher block. Insufficient depth here had been identified as the cause of the '77 failures. Against Porsche's four works cars (two four-valve 936/78s, a two-valve 936/77 and 'Moby Dick'), Renault ranged two A442s, an A442B with 2.0 litre engine and an A443 with enlarged, 2.1 version of the twin turbo V6. A novel feature of the team's revised aerodynamics was a bubble cockpit canopy which improved top speed but made the driver hot and claustrophobic.

The race proved that Porsche might have won pole by dipping below the circuit record of the 917 era, but Renault had been running closer to race potential. Worse for Porsche, at the end of the second lap both Ickx' four-valve pole car and Haywood's two-valver came into the pits for engine adjustment. Two laps later, more adjustment was required on each car. Out on the track, Wollek's four-valve car trailed the A443 of Jabouille and the A442B of Pironi, splitting the A442s. Schurti was running-in a new engine for Moby Dick and trailed the two-car Mirage team, which again was running Renault engines, but again lacked the pace of the factory cars.

It was three hours before Ickx/Pescarolo and Haywood/Gregg had sliced back through the mid-field runners. By that time the Mirage challenge had faded. One car was out with a broken alternator, the other had been delayed by electrical problems.

With four hours run, the race had established a firm pattern: the Jabouille/Depailler A443 a lap ahead of the Pironi/Jaussaud A442B, the

Porsche developed a four-valve version of its turbocharged flat 6 engine to meet the 1978 Renault challenge, but that was not enough... Photo: LAT.

Jarier/Bell A442 and the Wollek/Barth 936. Another lap back the Frequelin/Ragnotti/Dolhelm A442 was in the clutches of Schurti/Stommelen's Moby Dick 935 and the recovering Ickx/Pescarolo 936. The two-valve 936 had a further three laps deficit.

At 9.00 p.m. Ickx/Pescarolo lost fifth gear and, with it, 45 minutes. During that time the two-valve car came in for a 10 minute turbo change. With a quarter of the race run, Renault looked very strong but Porsche had one untroubled car and the decision was taken to put Ickx in it. By 1.30 a.m. it had moved into a strong second place...

During the early hours of Sunday morning Renault lost the Jarier/Bell A442 (broken transmission) but Jabouille/Depailler nursed a small but significant two-lap advantage over the Ickx 936. Behind, the remaining Renaults led the two-valve 936 while Moby Dick rounded out the top six. Mass had replaced Ickx in the other four-valve car and this lay eighth after electrical problems, while the surviving Mirage lay 19th after turbo and gear problems.

1978 was Renault's year. Here one of the Alpine-Renaults of the victorious works team leads one of the Renault-powered Mirages that provided a back-up for the strong French manufacturer. Photo: LAT.

The daylight hours brought more delays for the works Porsches... including a broken fifth gear for the second-placed 936. That cost 40 minutes, but no sooner were Jabouille/Depailler looking fair set for victory than the A443 holed a piston. With the Frequelin/Ragnotti/ Dolhelm A442 losing third gear, the midday leader board had a completely new look. Pironi/Jaussaud's A442B commanded an eight-lap margin over Ickx/Wollek/Barth, who had caught Haywood/Gregg, while the Frequelin/Ragnotti/Dolhelm A442 was three laps further adrift. Moby Dick had lost even more ground to engine trouble and the other four-valve car had crashed.

Ickx and company made a massive effort on Sunday afternoon, drawing out three laps on their team-mates. But the chase of the Renault was in vain – Porsche had to admit that this year Renault had been too strong for it. Stuttgart collected second and third places, while the other surviving Renault bagged fourth, eleven laps from the lead car, thanks to its gear breakage.

Even more unlucky was the troubled Mirage, which had to be content with 10th place, just a lap behind Jean Rondeau's GTP-winning effort. A development of the Inaltera-Cosworth (one of which ran privately and finished), the new Rondeau M378 GTP coupé crewed by Rondeau/ Darniche was not the fastest of the Cosworth entries but was the most rugged. It also outlasted a three-car WM-Peugeot team in claiming the GTP honours. Sadly, the last of the WMs was destroyed in a major crash on the Mulsanne, its driver lucky to escape with his life.

The Cosworth ranks had featured two new British cars, an Ibec-Hesketh 308LM based on the Hesketh Grand Prix car, and a new de Cadenet, developed from the team's modified Lola. Lacking proper testing, these new designs had been early pits visitors and had been bugged by problems throughout, as had an older de Cadenet car (the 75/6 Lola) which had been privately entered.

Once again Porsche 935s had collected high placings, thanks to prototype unreliability. Moby Dick fell to eighth due to its sick engine, but fifth, sixth and seventh places were filled by customer 935/77s, the leaders of a nine-car fleet which had shrugged off five less highly modified Ferrari 512BBs. It hadn't been a memorable race for the works Porsche team but the factory followed Renault's lead and announced its withdrawal from sports car racing. Renault looked to Grand Prix racing, Porsche to Indianapolis. Did the future for Le Mans really lie in that mixed bag of mid-field runners?

1.	2.0t Alpine-Renault* (Pironi/Jaussaud)	6.	3.0t Porsche* (Busby/Cord/Knoop)
2.	2.1t Porsche (Wollek/Barth/Ickx)		* Class winners. Also:
3.	2.1t Porsche (Haywood/Gregg/Joest)	9.	3.0 Rondeau (Rondeau/Darniche/Haran)
4.	2.0 Alpine-Renault (Frequelin/Ragnotti/Dolhelm)	11.	2.0 Chevron-Chrysler (Pignard/Rossiaud/Ferrier)
5.	3.0t Porsche* (Redman/Barbour/Paul)	12.	3.0 Porsche (Verney/Lapeyre/Servanin)

1979

On paper, the Cosworth Ford challenge had little more hope than in previous years. There might have been no Renaults present this year, but Porsche, contrary to its original plan, was back with two of its well-proven prototypes. Power was now claimed to be in excess of 600 b.h.p. (280 per litre). The top Cosworth tuners couldn't extract more than 450 b.h.p. without sacrificing 24-hour reliability. Little hope, then, for a repeat of the engine's '75 triumph, even if the Cluxton Mirages had reverted to Cosworth power.

In fact, the race presented a great opportunity to the Cosworth runners. Porsche's prototypes wilted within three hours of the start. Cluxton might have been denied the chance to retain his Renault engines and his revised 'Ford M10s' (with smaller frontal area and water cooled brakes) might have been 10 seconds off Porsche qualifying pace, but at the three-hour mark that didn't seem so important, after all. Sure, his Schuppan/Jaussaud entry was in the pits needing a gearbox change but the sister car of Bell/Hobbs was out front with only Porsche 935s for company. That type of Porsche it could cope with.

As evening drew in it looked good for Mirage, but with six-and-a-half hours' run the team's hopes sank. A broken exhaust took 27 minutes to repair. Like the Porsche prototypes, the Mirages could but spend the balance of the race attempting to recover...

Unlike the 936s, the Bell/Hobbs M10, into which Schuppan was drafted, at least saw the finish but well out of contention, having sustained bodywork damage following light failure and having lost first gear, then compression. A damaged piston cost its chance to cross the line in 16th position.

The second Mirage had been disqualified for losing too much ground to its gearbox change. However, the performance of the nine other Cosworth-powered prototypes had been little more impressive. Highest hopes had been held for Alain de Cadenet's revamped car, with longer

Porsche took its 936 back for one more try in 1979 thanks to a sponsorship offer by Essex Petroleum. In the absence of Renault, the two examples entered were the class of the field, but both hit trouble. Photo: LAT.

wheelbase, less weight and claimed handling and aerodynamic improvements. Alas, this fleet British challenger handled by de Cadenet/Migault tailed the Mirages for only five laps before it started losing oil. A faulty gearbox oil union spelt eventual retirement. Of three privately-entered Lola-DFVs of varying vintage, only one made the finish in 20th place and the first-ever serious Japanese team, which fielded two Cosworth challengers, fell by the wayside.

The oriental bid came in the form of two Dome Zero RLs: low, narrow, long tail cars with Alpine A443-style cockpit covers designed by Japanese Formula One designer Masao Ono with help from Len Bailey. Sadly, both British-based and managed cars were in the pits at the end of the first hour, one with head gasket failure.

The three other Cosworth-engined prototypes represented the main French hope. Constructor Jean Rondeau had prepared three evolutions of his '78 GTP car (with suspension and aerodynamic modifications), dubbed M379s, and had been rewarded with the prime paddock position, formerly granted to Matra, then Renault. His team repaid the compliment with a 10th place finish for its delayed Pescarolo/Beltoise entry and, better still, fifth place for Darniche/Ragnotti. That was the best that the Cosworth force made of its Great Opportunity.

For France, there were again three WM-Peugeots to cheer. This year the little team brought one of its slippery little coupés home 14th overall. All the French prototypes, like those of Britain, Japan, America, even Germany, were completely overwhelmed by 935 Porsches.

The event had promised to be a Porsche walkover from a few days before the closing date for entries, when the factory had put in its surprise two-car prototype entry. The team might have been busy with an Indianapolis project, but the offer of backing for another Le Mans bid from the mysterious Monaco-based oil tycoon David Thieme had been too much to resist, particularly as it opened up the possibility of a 'grand slam of long distance racing', 935 privateers having already won the two other round-the-clock classics, the Daytona 24-hours and Sebring 12-hours. Thieme, the multi-millionaire owner of Essex petroleum, was already co-sponsoring the Lotus Grand Prix team and a Porsche Le Mans bid clearly appealed to his ego. So it was that, despite having announced its withdrawal with the Renault pull-out, Porsche (in its own words), 'contrary to all expectations . . . once again fell in to compete in the year's most strenuous competition'.

To warm up for the classic, 936 chassis 001 was taken to the Silverstone Six-Hour race in May, where Mass/Redman were in a class of their own . . . until the car crashed at 170 m.p.h., perhaps due to a puncture. It was the second 936 in which Mass had suffered a major accident, but both of his wrecks were rebuilt with improved 600 b.h.p. engine – to dominate qualifying without any apparent effort.

The names of Ickx/Redman and Wollek/Haywood were at the top of the leaderboard, predictably, for the first two hours. Then came the first blows. Redman suffered a blow-out: the tyre flailed and damaged the bodywork. Wollek suffered a misfire. Ickx/Redman fell to 23rd position, Wollek/Haywood to sixth.

Within one hour Ickx had clawed back 10th place, and towards half distance the two fastest cars in the race were to be found in third and seventh positions. However, overnight there were more delays. Ickx had the ignition belt come off out on the circuit, then his team-mates suffered another misfire. Before three-quarter distance it had been announced that Ickx had been disqualified for receiving outside assistance: a mechanic had brought him the replacement belt.

At least the sister car was still in contention, and was catching the second-placed car (at this stage only a 935 privateer entry) despite a loss of compression in one cylinder. Alas, at 8.00 a.m. it gave up the ghost. By now the fragility of the prototypes had handed the race (run on Sunday in steady rain) to the silhouette cars.

Porsche's 1979 long-distance grand slam was completed by the Kremer brothers, who fielded the fastest 935 – to their own K3 twin turbo specification – for Ludwig/Whittington's B and D. There were some 13 935s running to either 'Group 5' or 'IMSA GTX' specification and the race came down to a duel between the fastest Group 5 car and the fastest IMSA example – Dick Barbour's, crewed by Stommelen/Barbour/Newman. Overnight the battle had been between Kremer and the arch-rival Loos team, but just after 4.00 a.m. Georg Loos' star driver Fitzpatrick rolled into the pits with his car enveloped in extinguisher foam – a turbo oil leak had caused the fire. A short while later the property magnate's second-placed entry rolled into the pits with a blown engine. That was it. Now the lead Kremer car lay a solid 12 laps ahead of the circumspect Barbour car, which was in the sights of the sick 936.

With the factory car gone and 15 laps between Kremer and Barbour it all looked over bar the shouting at 10.00 a.m., with just four hours still to run (the race having started at 2.00 p.m. this year). But the next hour brought drama: the Kremer car lost its injection pump belt. The best part of an hour was lost, which should have allowed Barbour into the lead. But his car lost time with a jammed wheel nut... at midday there was still a four lap margin. This became seven laps when a piston went with just 26 minutes to run. So it was that Porsche won... and lost. And resolved (once again) to leave the race to its privateers the following year.

1.	3.0t Porsche* (Ludwig/Whittington/Whittington)	5.	3.0 Rondeau-Ford* (Darniche/Ragnotti)
2.	3.0t Porsche* (Barbour/Newman/Stommelen)	6.	3.5 BMW (Winkelhock/Mignot/Poulain)
3.	3.0t Porsche (Ferrier/Trisconi/Servanin)		* Class winners. Also:
4.	3.0t Porsche* (Muller/Vanoli/Pallavicini)	14.	2.7 WM-Peugeot (Raulet/Mamers)
		17.	2.0 Chevron-Ford (Smith/Jones/Charnell)

138

1980

It was at the December 1979 Porsche 'Winners Ceremony' that it began. Marque Technical Director Helmut Bott gave Reinhold Joest – regular entrant of an old 908/3 prototype in 1000km races and long supporter of the company in endurance racing – the go-ahead to race an ex-factory 936 at Le Mans, in the absence of the works team from the prototype category. While the factory concentrated on a low-key programme proving a production 924 turbo, Joest would receive a 1977 two-valve engine equipped 936 that could reasonably be expected to be the class of a poor field.

For 1980 Le Mans had instigated a maximum fuel tank size of 120 litres and a refuelling flow rate that would keep cars in the pits for around two minutes, so fuel economy became a major consideration. The two-valve flat-six would provide an economical, dependable 550 b.h.p. – 100 b.h.p. more than any of its Ford-powered rivals – and the prospects for Joest's self-prepared car were rosy enough to tempt Ickx out of 'retirement' for a crack at compatriot Gendebien's joint four wins. This really would be his last race, he promised.

The opposition certainly was weak – in the absence of the Mirage team only six Cosworth-powered prototypes would face the Porsche, along with three WM-Peugeots. The Cosworth cars consisted of three Rondeaux, the de Cadenet, a Dome and a new shape in the form of an ACR (Andre Chevalley Racing) from Geneva, based, like the de Cadenet, on a Lola T380 chassis.

Jean Rondeau's entries once again held the prime paddock site and this year really were a force to be reckoned with – qualifying was based on the average time recorded by all a car's drivers and Pescarolo/ Ragnotti wrapped up pole for the local team. Their car was an M379B, a development of the '79 car with improved cooling and longer rear bodywork that had undergone a 26-hour reliability run at the Circuit Paul Ricard without trouble.

Not that the Joest-run Porsche was outrun. It was the faster machine and Ickx was content simply to keep it in contention in the early, wet stages of the race. Almost four hours had elapsed before it moved into the lead, seemingly destined for its inevitable victory. However, at 9.30 p.m. Ickx suffered a broken fuel injection belt – a repeat of the previous year's failure. This year there was a spare on board and less than half an hour was lost. After six hours the car lay sixth and by the 12-hour mark it was in the lead once more, one lap ahead of the Rondeau/Jaussaud Rondeau:

the Pescarolo/Ragnotti example had retired with head gasket failure.

Once ahead again, Ickx/Joest held a steady pace – but didn't stay out of trouble. At 9.55 a.m., fifth gear stripped and Rondeau/Jaussaud sailed past. The Porsche lost 25 minutes to the French hope, but with one hour still to run was less than two laps behind. With 40 minutes to run, Ickx unlapped the car – but catching up a complete lap in the time left was a daunting proposition. The Belgian had only just buckled down to the task when the heavens opened. He dived into the pits. The Rondeau stayed out on slicks. Quickly the shower stopped and the line dried: the glory of France was assured.

Behind Ickx/Joest the third Rondeau, in heavier GTP trim, took a good solid third place (and the class win) so the home team had plenty to be joyful about. It was also a constructive weekend for the improving little WM team, based at Thorigny near Paris. The Gerard Welter/Michel Meunier-entered cars had been extensively modified following wind tunnel tests and their Peugeot PRV V6 engines were now reckoned to produce 500 b.h.p. at race boost. One of the narrow track machines recorded the fastest Mulsanne speed of practice at 217 m.p.h. and, despite a troubled race, Frequelin/Dorchy came home a splendid fourth overall. The team also collected 11th place and suffered just one retirement.

In contrast, it was another heartache 24-hours for the de Cadenet team, which had won the Monza and Silverstone 1000km races earlier in the season. The team's essentially unchanged-from-'79-specification car was extensively damaged in practice. Having been rebuilt for the race, it suffered electrical mishaps in the early stages, from which it did well to recover during the night, to the extent that it looked set for a top-three placing when it suffered a broken rear cross member early on Sunday morning. Crewed by de Cadenet/Migault, the gallant British hope finished seventh. At least it survived: the ACR didn't, and the new Dome Zero RL80 (with reshaped bodywork and wider track for better stability) never overcame a gearbox rebuild during the first four hours: it took the flag in 25th and last position.

This year the highest silhouette car was in fifth place. It was a Dick Barbour entry to the latest Kremer K3/80 specification. Overnight it had run with the leaders, outpacing the other Group 5/GTX entries. Loss of compression in one cylinder cost its hopes of a stronger finish. This year didn't belong to the production-style cars – it belonged to a coupé prototype that pointed the way to the future of endurance cars, while making history for France.

1.	3.0 Rondeau-Ford* (Rondeau/Jaussaud)	6.	2.0t Porsche (Barth/Schurti/Braun)
2.	2.1t Porsche (Ickx/Joest)		* Class winners. Also:
3.	3.0 Rondeau-Ford* (Spice/Martin/Martin)	8.	3.0t Porsche (Schornstein/Grohs/von Tschirnhaus)
4.	2.7 WM-Peugeot (Frequelin/Dorchy)	16.	3.0 Porsche (Perrier/Carmillet)
5.	3.2t Porsche* (Fitzpatrick/Redman/Barbour)	17.	Chevron-ROC (Hesnault/Sotty/Laurent)

1981

Rondeau's Cosworth-propelled double victory bid could but be an optimistic one. On the 30th anniversary of its first-ever Le Mans entry, Porsche was back – with a new, plus 600 b.h.p. turbo engine. The prospect of Group C regulations sweeping aside silhouette GTs in 1982 had enticed the factory. The new prototype formula would impose a fuel ration as an alternative to a capacity limit and, in the light of the consumption this would call for, Porsche reckoned that a 2.65 litre version of its familiar four-valve flat-six should do very nicely. Such an engine had been developed for Indy Car racing to produce over 700 b.h.p. on methanol and the conversion back to petrol was a fairly straightforward job. In essence the unit was a larger capacity version of the regular 2.1 litre flat-six: the only real differences were welded cylinder heads and alternative valve angles. However, it had a better bore/stroke ratio from the point of view of balance and needed only 1.3 bar boost to produce in excess of 600 b.h.p. Well within its capability, it hadn't missed a beat during a 31-hour computer-simulated Le Mans test on the rolling road.

Lifting of the prototype 3.0 litre capacity restriction for the last year of the category gave Porsche the chance to run its intended Group C engine at Le Mans for real, in a 936 chassis. Sure, the 936 design was now over five years old (and of spaceframe rather than monocoque construction) but there had been little development in the interim to worry the Weissach engineers and they took the chassis out of the museum secure in the knowledge that it would have plenty of power over the opposition.

Sure enough, the 936s didn't have to try in qualifying. Dusted down and equipped with new wings plus the potent new drivetrain (feeding through a four-speed Can Am transmission rated at 1000 b.h.p.), they were the class of the field. No special effort was needed to leave the Rondeau team five seconds behind. Pole went to Ickx/Bell, the Belgian ace coming out of 'retirement' once more (saying 'only a fool never changes his mind') to request the Englishman as his team-mate. The second car lined up alongside had been entrusted to Mass/Schuppan/Haywood. The closest challenger on grid times was Joest's 936, still with a regular 2.1 litre engine and this year handled by its owner/Whittington/Niedzwiedz.

The Joest car kept in contention in the early stages despite a power deficit of more than 50 b.h.p., but the factory wasn't about to rush things ... At any rate, at the five-hour mark the gallant private effort came to an end following an argument with a barrier. Thereafter, the

After a one-year absence, the Porsche 936 was back in 1981, this time with a 2.65 litre engine intended for the following year's Group C formula. This is the Ickx/Bell winning example which found no real opposition once its sister car had run into trouble. Photo: John Overton.

factory didn't need to look over its shoulder. And, although originally intended for 500-mile races, the 'Indy' engine in the Ickx/Bell car didn't miss a beat. Not once did the team need to lift the engine cover, and not once did the chassis cause concern. Ickx took an unprecedented fifth win in unflustered style. Mind you, Bell couldn't resist some fast laps right at the end, just for fun . . . and proceeded to collapse on the victory balcony!

Sadly, the second works Porsche wasn't able to follow its sister home to a triumphant one-two. Its problems had started soon after the 3.00 p.m. off, taking the dubious honour of first pits visitor, thanks to a broken plug ceramic. After charging up to second place, the clutch gave trouble, later the fuel injection system played up. Having lost 40 laps to its victorious sister, it finished an unlucky 13th.

Unlucky, too, was the Rondeau team, which lost a car and a driver on Saturday evening. The Lafosse/Ragnotti car had a brief off-road excursion at the hands of the former, damaging its splitter. Then turned sharp right at 160 m.p.h. while accelerating up the Mulsanne, to claim the life of its driver. With four other cars in the running, the team resolved to continue, as Lafosse would surely have wished.

Two of the Cosworth-powered French challengers (379Cs with revised aerodynamics for a better Mulsanne top speed) were equipped with a 3.3 'DFL' version of the familiar Formula One engine. This had been developed by Cosworth as the first step in Ford's Group C involvement, which would embrace a Ford C100 prototype to chase 1982 World Endurance Championship honours. Despite the 10% capacity boost, the impressively torquey engine's 520 b.h.p. power output was light years away from that of Porsche's (very comfortably blown) projected Group C engine. Already Cosworth knew that turbocharging would have to be the answer, in spite of widespread lobbying for a formula to limit power to the region of 500/550 b.h.p. Cosworth's enlarged bore motor also powered de Cadenet's old Lola and a new, Group C-destined Lola T600 coupé. The marque's first fully enclosed sports-racing car since its classic T70 design (thanks to the Group C stipulations), this was the first Le Mans prototype to exploit the potential of Formula One type ground effect technology.

Group C would call for coupés having a flat bottom area of at least 800mm × 1000mm, but around this there would be no restriction on the production of ground effect through underbody venturi shapes. The Lola had tunnels running either side of its mandatory flat surface and created plenty of downforce, but was disappointingly slow on the Mulsanne – probably as a penalty of its new technology. Of the 3.3 DFL-equipped challengers it was the only one to see the finish. Crewed by Edwards/de Villota/Fernandez, it overcame many mishaps, including the engine shaking the exhaust system to pieces, to take 15th place.

Both lead Rondeaus (10 seconds faster this year but frustratingly off Porsche pace) suffered fuel pump drive failures which cost over an hour in the pits, and the Pescarolo/Tambay example subsequently became stranded out on the circuit due to a flat battery. The Rondeau/Jaussaud sister car finally retired at midnight with an unfathomable handling malady, after suffering gearbox problems. Nevertheless, the team's two 3.0 litre DFV-engined back-up cars kept the Ford flag flying and Haran/Schlesser/Streiff plugged on to a rousing second overall, 14 laps adrift, in spite of a stripped gear on Sunday afternoon. In the other car, Spice/Migault cursed two ignition changes that dropped them from second to third.

While Rondeau salvaged a very respectable result for France and Ford, the all-French WM-Peugeot team, benefiting from fresh, factory-developed four valve heads that pushed power over 500 b.h.p., suffered two shunts on the Mulsanne, from which their drivers were lucky to escape uninjured, plus a fire. The team could manage no better than 14th for its surviving car, which overcame a broken front wishbone.

Aside from the Porsche, Rondeau, Lola and WM prototypes, this was another year of Group 5/GTX GT car conflict. Apart from some excitement generated by the return of the Porsche 917. Group C regulations called for fully enclosed bodywork once more and while the factory proved its intended engine, it also helped a project to race a replica of the last Porsche coupé, the 917K. This was undertaken by the Kremer brothers, who were supplied with original engines on the condition that they stuck to the original chassis concept – albeit allowed the liberty of lowering the bodywork and adding a rear wing. Sadly, this refresher course in the design of coupé bodywork was handicapped by a lack of test mileage. The 12-cylinder engine proved to be starved of air to the extent that the recreated old warrior was over 50 m.p.h. slower on the Mulsanne than the 936/81 – or, indeed, the *langhecks* of its day. It managed to nudge into the top 10 before breaking its chassis in an accident, after seven hours' toil.

In Group 5/GTX, the 2.0 litre Group 5 division was a straightforward affair for Lancia: the factory lost two of its weakly-opposed 1.4 litre turbocharged Beta Montecarlos but brought the survivors home eighth and 16th overall to record its first Le Mans finish. However, the over-2.0 litre action saw Ferrari come close to upsetting the form book, after hopes of a three-way contest had been dashed by the unreliability of the low-on-power 3.5 litre BMW M1s. The 475 b.h.p. of BMW's unblown straight-six was insufficient to concern Porsche. Ferrari had no more engine power, but the staying power to get a result...

The most potent Porsche in the field was a Kremer-run 3.2 litre 935K3 with the latest (800 b.h.p. potential) factory engine kit. Driven by Field/Whittington/Whittington, it had its moment of glory in the early stages, but it might well have been exploiting too much of its potential for comfort, for after five hours of impressive progress its flat six cried enough.

More reasonable speed for solid reliability was demonstrated by the older, British-based 935K3 of Cooper/Wood/Bourgoigne, which came home fourth overall, a mere two laps clear of the surprise of the race: the splendid Pozzi Ferrari 512BB crewed by veteran Frenchmen Andruet/Ballot-Lena. This in turn was but a single lap ahead of the only other K3 in the race to use the latest engine kit, the Daytona 24-hours' winning 3.2 litre Cooke-Woods' entry.

Fifth overall (first in GTX) was the best-ever result for Ferrari's mid-engined Seventies supercar. The 512BB wasn't an obvious base for a race car, thanks to the transverse and over-the-gearbox placement of its flat-12 engine and it had only ever been expected to tackle the Daytona and Le Mans marathons. The car hadn't been officially developed for competition by the factory but Gaetano Florini of the marque's 'Assistenza Clienti' had handed out help to concessionaires and others through the back door.

The 512BB engine could only be lightly tuned to 465 b.h.p., for that was all the gearbox could stand and lightening, suspension and aerodynamic modifications could do little to overcome the car's disadvantageous layout. Nevertheless, a good example pounded the Mulsanne at over 200 m.p.h. and the strong top six position by Pozzi after a faster NART car had fallen out was a great credit to Florini's efforts. But the Maranello marque hadn't halted Porsche's six-year rout of silhouette racing. With Group C looming, could Ford do anything to stop the Black Horse of Stuttgart galloping to further glory?

1.	2.6t Porsche* (Ickx/Bell/Barth)	6.	3.1t Porsche (Verney/Garretson/Cooke)
2.	3.0 Rondeau-Ford* (Haran/Schlesser/Streiff)		* Class winners. Also:
3.	3.0 Rondeau-Ford (Spice/Migault)	11.	2.0t Porsche (Rouse/Schurti)
4.	3.1t Porsche* (Cooper/Wood/Bourgoignie)	17.	3.0 Porsche (Bertapelle/Perrier/Salam)
5.	4.9 Ferrari* (Andruet/Ballot-Lena)	18.	2.0 Lola-BMW (Grand/Courage)

1982

The race, revitalized by the new Group C regulations, was billed as Ford versus Porsche. By half distance it was no contest. Ford's backing for a bigger displacement version of Cosworth's ultra-successful 3.0 litre DFV Formula One engine did not look auspicious as the 3950cc DFL-engined cars fell out one by one with engine or engine-associated problems. Meanwhile, the Stuttgart steamroller swept on, propelled by its more powerful, more fuel efficient power plant – the superb four-valve water-cooled head version of the classic flat six. Porsche's first Group C car – its first monocoque race car, its first ground effect race car – might have been 60kgs over the 800kg minimum weight and, some suggested, over-engineered, but it did everything asked of it while the opposition fell apart in its wheeltracks.

Group C called for no obvious technical solution. The regulations simply imposed a fuel ration of 2600 litres for a 24-hour race, with a maximum of 25 fuel stops and a maximum fuel tank capacity of 100 litres, to be refuelled at a maximum flow rate of 50 litres per minute. Burn that however you wish, provided your choice of engine carries the name of a mass car manufacturer. Porsche knew from its experience the previous year that the 2.65 litre version of its four-valve flat-six was an excellent answer. As soon as the Group C regulations had been confirmed, Cosworth had known that its proposed long stroke 3.95 litre development of the 3.3 DFL would need turbocharging to take advantage of all the available fuel, and that was a development which would take time. So the first Ford versus Porsche contest was a rather unequal one.

The new Porsche 956 Group C car showed its class right from the start of practice. Turning its wheels for the first time in anger, within no time Ickx' example was under the lap record. Pole position was secured early on in the proceedings with a time a fraction quicker than the 936/81 had managed, without resorting to qualifying tyres. And that was despite a 16 m.p.h. slower top speed, thanks to the coupé bodywork compulsory for Group C and higher drag ground effect aerodynamics. Porsche's 911-sired flat-six ran 1.2 bar in qualifying, good for 615 b.h.p. and 1.1 bar in the race: a conservative 590 b.h.p. No other prototype had that sort of power (the Ford engine offering no more than 540 b.h.p., for example) and no other chassis could match the 956's combination of good speed on the Mulsanne (Ickx was fastest through the speed trap) and downforce aided grip through the corners.

To comply with new Group C regulations Porsche developed the 956 prototype with 2.65 litre turbocharged engine and coupé body which exploited the potential of underbody 'ground effect' air tunnelling. Here the winning example of Ickx/Bell leads the sister car of Mass/Schuppan which finished second as part of a convincing display of Stuttgart supremacy. Photo: John Overton.

Mass secured the front row for Porsche (Ickx was sharing with Bell, Mass with Schuppan), but a third works car for Holbert/Haywood languished back on row seven due to a gremlin in its braking system. All three cars were brand new for the meeting. The prototype, which had raced once, at Silverstone, languished under a tarpaulin. It had successfully completed a 24-hour computer-simulated rolling road Le Mans test before the three replicas had been constructed for the race.

Race the 956s certainly did, but only during the opening stages of the event. The Ford-powered opposition forced a sprint race pace from the start, and the number one and number two Porsches flew the flag up front until the first round of pit stops after 47 minutes, all three works cars coming in on the same lap, before the Cosworth cars. Ickx stopped again 51 minutes later to hand over to Bell, who was given strict instructions to 'cool it'. Fuel consumption was of paramount consideration.

Considerations of fuel consumption were still to the fore when Ickx unexpectedly swept into the pits at 9.30 the following morning, three laps ahead of schedule. Throughout the hours of darkness, while the breathless opposition had crumbled, the lead factory Porsche had performed faultlessly. The greatest worry had been a misfire between 6000 and 7000 r.p.m. – cured by simply richening the mixture. Now the worry was something strange about the handling. It was a puncture that the Belgian driver had sensed as he had negotiated the Ford chicane immediately before the pits, and his quick perception of trouble had saved having to run for a lap on it. But the question was, could the 956 be refuelled three laps early?

The pace of the number one car certainly had been cooled after that second pit stop. Careful driving had kept the car well within the 107 litres/hour consumption rate calculated to make the finish with a small margin for safety. Digital cockpit readouts were keeping the drivers aware of the consumption rate they were achieving: both Ickx and Bell complained that this 'race' was more like an economy run. But they had built up a sufficient margin to be able to stop three laps early. They had not been unduly concerned when the more aggressively driven number three car had forged ahead during the night and had become firmly established in front after both sister cars had hit snags . . .

The Holbert/Haywood car lost the lead at 12.30 a.m. when a door flew off, costing 20 minutes in the pits. Later the car stopped for wheel and suspension problems, dropping as low as ninth overall, 21 laps behind, early Sunday morning. At this stage factory test driver Barth was brought in to reinforce the driving strength and, by Sunday lunchtime, having made up two laps of its deficit, the car was in third place. Meanwhile, the number two Porsche had lost two laps due to a faulty rev limiter and a blocked fuel filter. With half-an-hour to run the three Stuttgart runners lined up astern in numerical and race order, to cruise home to a triumphant finish – which they never quite made as the crowd swarmed onto the track at 4.00 p.m., blocking the finish line.

In beating the 936/81's winning average, despite the economy measures, Ickx/Bell won the ACO's Thermal Index of Efficiency. And well deserved it was, too.

Porsche not only took the top three positions, but made a clean sweep of the top five. Fourth overall was a 'Moby Dick' replica, built by Reinhold Joest and run by John Fitzpatrick for himself and Hobbs. With the 956 not on public sale, Fitzpatrick reckoned that a 935-powered Moby Dick was the next best thing – quick on the straight and certain to pick up places as the Cosworth Group C runners hit trouble. Sure enough, the sweet-running IMSA GTX category machine (not until 1983 would the race be confined to the new Groups B and C) had moved into the top six by half distance, thanks to the fragility of the faster Group C cars, and hopes ran high. Alas, at 6.15 a.m. Fitzpatrick brought it in with a blown head gasket. Some sterling work by the crew isolated the number three cylinder and kept the car going on five – strongly enough to finish. Which was some consolation for constructor Joest, whose own Group C car lost a potential third place when it retired close to the end.

Both Joest and arch-rival Kremer entered one-off Porsche-based Group C specials for the event. Kremer went for a strikingly shaped chassis, with some 936 parts, powered by a 2.8 litre, 935 twin turbo motor, Joest for what was esentially a coupé version of a 936 chassis with 2.5 litre twin turbo two valve engine.

The cars differed greatly in the amount of development they had enjoyed – Joest's had raced at Monza, Silverstone and the Nurburgring; Kremer's was new for the event, as the previous year's 917 had been. The Joest '936C' in the hands of Wollek and the *frères* Martin, qualified on the second row, just a fraction slower than the 'well within potential' 956s, while the Kremer 'CK-5', entrusted to Ongias/Field/Whittington, was some six seconds slower. A bigger margin came in relative race performance – the Kremer car retired during the second hour (driveshaft failure) while the Joest machine went on and on.

The performance of the 936C was most commendable. It kept the works car on their toes throughout the hours of darkness, while the rest of the C car entry crumbled. Come Sunday afternoon and it had a three-lap margin over the badly delayed third works car (and the speed not to lose that) when the engine blew.

So it was that of 29 C cars which had started the race, only three finished strongly. In contrast to the fragility of the new generation, 18 old-style IMSA GTX/Group 5 cars started and nine finished, with the Fitzpatrick Porsche followed home by a Kremer 935K3 crewed by Snobeck/Servanin/Metge (which was likewise running on less than six cylinders). The highest non-Porsche at the finish was third in the IMSA GTX class: the Ferrari 512BB of Dieudonne/Baird/Liebert. A similar NART car in the hands of Cudini/Morton/Paul Senior had vied with the Fitzpatrick car for the GTX lead overnight and had looked set to take the class when it expired a few hours from home.

Porsche and Ferrari carved up the top nine places between themselves, with the exception of a lone Aston Martin Nimrod, which came home seventh. Two of these British-built Group C cars had started the race, almost two decades after the Aston Martin factory had last contested it. The return was brought about through the enthusiasm of company Chairman Victor Gauntlett and dealer Robin Hamilton, who got together to form Nimrod Racing Automobiles with the aim of promoting a 5.3 litre V8 Aston Martin-engined C car. The factory's Tickford engineering offshoot developed the 5340cc two-valve d.o.h.c., 90 degree vee stock block power house to produce an encouraging 570 b.h.p. and Lola's Eric Broadley was commissioned to design a suitable chassis. Broadley produced a flat bottom car (almost a Lola T70 derivative) which was slippery and rugged, but overweight. Both the works entry (Needell/Lees/Evans) and a works supported car run by Ray Mallock for Viscount Downe (Mallock/Salmon/Phillips) tipped the scales at something in excess of 1000kgs. The cars qualified in mid-field. Sadly, the works machine got away from Needell when it started fishtailing on the Mulsanne early in the race. Needell had cause to thank its inherent strength.

That same strength saw the other example pound its way up the lap chart from 23rd on the grid to sixth with six hours run. Battleship sturdy, it continued its progress overnight, not a threat to the leading 956s, but on course to beat the delayed third car – until its engine went off song with four hours to run. The problem steadily got worse but at least it saw the end.

In contrast to Aston Martin's 50% finishing record and praiseworthy seventh place, the best Cosworth-Ford could muster was two finishers from 18 starters, the highest in 10th place. And that car was using a conventional 3.0 litre DFV. A serious vibration problem afflicted the long stroke DFL. Rondeau Team Manager Keith Greene suggested that at least one of his three 382s (a development of the familiar 379) should run a dependable 3.0 litre engine, but all his drivers wanted to go for glory with the extra 60 b.h.p. offered by the 3.95 DFL, despite worries over the vibration of the engine. A similar philosophy saw the new wing cars from

Ford (the Len Bailey-designed C100) and Lola (the Broadley-penned T610 – a development of his T600) identically equipped, each concern running two entries.

Of the three marques spearheading the Ford challenge, only the Lola, its aerodynamics developed in the Williams Grand Prix team's wind tunnel-equipped facility, could match Porsche's Mulsanne speed. The marque had learnt the lesson of the T600 and in the early stages the Edwards/Keegan T610 had a good dice with the 956s. Things started going wrong in the second hour when the doors started belling and it dropped right out of contention, eventually to retire with head gasket failure. The second Lola retired during the third hour due to a miscalculation over fuel.

An hour-and-a-half later the Ford C100 of Ludwig/Surer stopped with terminal electrical problems: this had been the quickest Cosworth-Ford car in practice, despite a relative lack of top speed, and for five hours it had kept with the leaders, which had included its sister car. However, the Winkelhock/Neidzweidz machine had been in clutch trouble from the second hour onwards and its engine expired after six hours. Things were looking bleak for Ford, particularly as both of the neat, fast 3.9 DFL-powered Sauber wing cars from Germany had fallen by the wayside due to the engine vibration problem.

As darkness shrouded the circuit only the Rondeau team carried the hopes of Ford. The first French challenger fell by the wayside soon after midnight. However, at least one of its sister cars was still in contention, keeping the hopes of the partisan crowd alive. Alas, at 2.15 a.m. it was all over – both remaining cars coasted to a halt at Arnage with electrical failure caused by engine vibrations, within moments of each other.

Mind you, Group C unreliability wasn't confined to the Ford representatives. Two rapid WM-Peugeots (no longer works supported) fell out, as did two new ground effect Marches powered by the old 5.7 litre V8 Chevrolet engine. And appalling reliability wasn't confined to Group C. Lancia had built small, fleet 1.4 litre turbocharged ground effect prototype spyders to chase the *drivers'* World Championship and, lighter and more nimble than Group C cars, these devices had proved surprisingly effective at circuits as diverse as Silverstone and the Nurburgring. But at Le Mans they were both sitting by the side of the track within 15 minutes of the start. All of which went to underline the excellence of those 956s from Weissach...

1.	2.6t Porsche* (Ickx/Bell)	6.	4.9 Ferrari (Dieudonne/Baird/Liebert)
2.	2.6t Porsche (Mass/Schuppan)		* Class winners. Also:
3.	2.6t Porsche (Haywood/Holbert/Barth)	8.	3.1t Porsche (Cooper/Smith/Bougoignie)
4.	3.1t Porsche* (Fitzpatrick/Hobbs)	13.	3.0t Porsche (Dron/Cleare/Jones)
5.	3.1t Porsche (Snobeck/Servanin/Metge)	16.	2.0t Porsche (Busby/Bundy)

1983

Prior to the race a French newspaper exclaimed: 'Lancia pour le spectacle, Rondeau pour le coeur – Porsche pour le logique'', which rather neatly summarized the situation. Lancia's new LC2 Group C car was fast enough to take a front row grid position but the marque didn't seriously expect its three entries to last – Spa in September was Team Manager Cesare Fiorio's target for race competitiveness. The new Rondeau M482 wing cars had the problematical Cosworth 3.95 DFL engine – without the planned turbocharger in the wake of Ford's decision to pull out of endurance racing. Driven flat out, the French cars wouldn't use up the 2,600 litre fuel ration. Porsche's superb 956 race car was logically once again in a class of its own.

On paper, the Lancia LC2 was a real threat to Stuttgart's supremacy, thanks to a brand new (Dunlop shod) ground effect monocoque chassis and a Ferrari-based 2.65 litre, four valves per cylinder d.o.h.c. V8 turbo engine developed by Abarth to produce 640 b.h.p. – the sort of figure Porsche was using this year. The car was not grossly overweight but early season races at Monza, Silverstone and the Nurburgring had shown that development time was lacking and a switch from Pirelli radials had been made in mid-stream. The front row position for star drivers Alboreto and Fabi was a great boost for the new-to-C1 team, but staying up among the Porsches was another matter altogether. Sure enough, after only one hour any semblance of a challenge had faded. Gear linkage, fuel pump, fuel feed: the breakages continued through the night. All three cars retired.

By 1983 Group C was well established with a variety of competing marques but no real threat to Porsche. Here the winning third-string 956 laps a Dome, one of the many Cosworth-powered prototypes which failed to provide stiff opposition. Photo: John Overton.

Rondeau was no luckier, although the team was fortunate to be competing at all. Desperately short of finance, Ford France had stepped in at the last moment with backing for a three-car effort using the unproven 482 ground effect design. Alas, it turned out to be short of speed and prone to porpoising on the long chute, where the bumps were incompatible with the hard springs necessary to get the best out of the high download design on the bends. The car had too much downforce, too much drag and, worse still, was underpowered. Unblown, a 3.95 DFL could muster little more than 570 b.h.p. And the unreliability was still with it. All three cars retired with broken engines.

Three old Rondeau 382s were in private hands and, equipped with 3.3 DFL engines, two of these finished, in 19th and 20th places. Both 3.3 and 3.95 Cosworth-Ford engines were used in a variety of other chassis including Dome, Grid, de Cadenet, Cougar, Sehcar, Lola and Ford (ex-works C100) but 19th and 20th places were the only finishes.

Aston Martin Tickford again fared better than Cosworth, but this year its best result was only 17th. The company had modified its 5.3 litre V8 at the cost of some £100,000 to make it lighter, more powerful and suitable for use as a stressed member in a new Len Bailey-designed, Steve O'Rourke-financed, Michael Cane Racing-run chassis christened the EMKA. This brand-new challenger, which employed a modest amount of ground effect, badly lacked development miles but overcame a holed radiator and broken suspension at least to finish, unlike the solitary Nimrod.

The works Nimrod team having run out of funds, the Nimrod representative was Viscount Downe's C2B, modified and lightened by Ray Mallock but still far too heavy, and underpowered, for all Tickford's efforts. In any case the engine broke.

Entries like the Cosworth-Ford and Aston Martin cars, the WM-Peugeots (one finish in 16th place; one retirement) or the 3.5 litre BMW straight-six-engined cars (a URD which retired and a Sauber which finished a splendid ninth), were no more than make-weights in C1 this year. With the early demise of Lancia (and the failure of Rondeau to live up to the hopes of the nation) the race was a clean sweep for Porsche and the 956 took the top eight places, surpassing Ferrari's record of filling the top six.

The 956 having proved its superiority in 1982, the factory had built a batch of 12 customer cars to late '82 specification and all had been snapped up, despite a hefty price tag. The buyers included some of the world's leading sports car entrants such as Reinhold Joest, the Kremer brothers and John Fitzpatrick, and Joest had caused a major surprise by beating the factory fair and square in the opening round of the 1983 World Endurance Championship at Monza. The factory had responded by improving its Bosch Motronic engine management system equipped power plant to make it more fuel-efficient than the mechanical injection customer engines and was in a class of its own at the subsequent races: Silverstone, the Nurburgring... and Le Mans.

Nevertheless, 1983 saw a thrilling finish, all the same. In addition to regular runners Ickx/Bell and Mass/Bellof, the works again fielded a third car for Holbert/Haywood/Schuppan and it was the number three car in front at the end. Mass/Bellof retired overnight with a broken engine and Ickx/Bell suffered a major setback when their car rolled to a halt with a dead engine. Luckily Bell was able to bring it back to life using the on-board Motronics repair kit, but the number three car had the break. The twist came right at the end of the day, when the leading car's door blew out. Ickx had been due to take the last stint in the pursuing number one car but had judged it too risky to continue without a change of pads. Bell had accepted the risk and the blown-out door helped put him onto the lead lap. Worse befell Holbert starting the last lap: the lack of a door had disrupted the air flow to the cylinder head water radiator and the engine seized solid. Somehow it restarted, and its air cooled block saw it to the finish, little more than a minute ahead of Bell's magnificent, charging effort...

With Holbert limping over the line and Bell finishing with insufficient fuel to go another lap, the race could so easily have fallen to the top private 956, six laps down but running strongly. This was a Kremer entry, for Andretti Senior and Junior and Alliot, which had enjoyed a trouble-free run and had inherited third soon after midnight. It held third, even second when Ickx/Bell dropped back, to the end, averaging close to the winning speed until midday when the car had to be slowed due to lack of fuel. The Motronic system was the winners' edge.

Still, almost all the customer 956s lasted. Joest's second entry in the hands of Merl/Schickentanz/de Narvaez was another trouble-free runner: it finished three laps adrift of the Kremer car to claim fourth place. Those customer cars pushed hard suffered a number of component failures. Without a massive factory-size budget a customer team cannot afford to change components as frequently, so has to test component reliability to a higher degree. Richard Lloyd's Canon team suffered heavily in this respect. However, the only one of the eight customer 956s to fall by the wayside was the fastest Fitzpatrick entry (Hobbs/Quester/Fitzpatrick), on which the metering unit broke. Fitzpatrick then joined Edwards and Keegan in his second car and finished fifth, ahead of Joest's troubled number one entry (Wollek/Ludwig) which was hampered by a misfire for two hours, blown out windows and a shunt which necessitated a rear end rebuild.

If nothing else, the ruggedness of the 956 would be worthy of praise. But when such a car is also the class of a world class field, it really is something rather special.

1.	2.6t Porsche*	5.	2.6t Porsche
	(Holbert/Haywood/Schuppan)		(Edwards/Keegan/Fitzpatrick)
2.	2.6t Porsche	6.	2.6t Porsche
	(Ickx/Bell)		(Ludwig/Wollek/Johansson)
3.	2.6t Porsche		* Class winner. Also:
	(Andretti/Andretti/Alliot)	11.	3.3t Porsche
4.	2.6t Porsche		(Cooper/Smith/Ovey)
	(Merl/de Narvaez/Schickentanz)	12.	1.3 Mazda
			(Katayama/Terada/Yorino)

1984

Lancia had a golden opportunity at Le Mans in 1984. The Porsche works team was absent – it withdrew its entry in protest at a sudden FISA decision to scrap the Group C fuel economy formula in favour of an IMSA-style sliding scale equating engine type and capacity with minimum weight for 1985. This move was influenced by the ACO's desire to attract entries from the American IMSA prototype series. However, it was a move which would waste a vast investment in engine management technology made in anticipation of a tighter fuel economy formula by both Porsche and Lancia. Porsche felt that enough was enough. Lancia may well have taken a similar stand, but for pressure from its sponsors. The fact that it didn't, meant that it faced a Le Mans without its greatest rival.

It was a race to be run under the same 2,600 litre fuel ration as in '83 – a proposed 15% reduction had been postponed in the light of FISA's radical proposals for 1985 – and at a 50kgs higher minimum weight, which suited Lancia as its cars were around 850kgs in any case – the Porsches would have to be ballasted.

Lancia faced a formidable army of privately-run 956s as its serious opposition. Despite losing its Chief Engineer, Giovanni Tonti, to the Alfa Romeo Grand Prix bid, its preparations were very thorough and included the readying of a bored-out version of its Ferrari V8 engine with a capacity 17% greater (just over 3.0 litres), said to produce 680 b.h.p. Endurance trials were carried out at Monza and Mugello and the Italians even went as far as simulating the Mulsanne straight on the runways of Caselle Turin Airport.

The Porsche factory's boycott of the 1984 race handed Lancia a golden opportunity. The Italian marque's turbocharged LC2 prototype was now well sorted yet failed to find the 24-hour reliability needed to match a competitive pace. Photo: John Overton.

Using the normal (640 b.h.p. in race trim) 2.65 litre engine and Dunlop qualifying tyres, the Lancia team comfortably wrapped up the front row of the grid, although Wollek was frustrated that traffic had cost his chance of breaking Ickx' qualifying record en route to pole. He shared the lead car with Nannini while Barilla/Baldi/Heyer crewed the sister entry which lined up alongside. The 3.0 litre engine was installed for the race, but kept a closely-guarded secret. However, the fact that the team's Hewland-based Abarth gearbox was a weak link in its chain (one had broken during trials at Monza, for example), was widely appreciated. Still, even if the cars didn't last, with the bigger engine they could well hope to do plenty of leading, and that would be a boost to the morale of a team that had suffered more than its fair share of bad luck.

But lead Wollek didn't on lap one. Cheeky WM-Peugeot team owner Roger Dorchy turned his V6 turbo's boost up high and used his narrow track, flat bottom car's prodigious Mulsanne speed to seize the initiative, to the delight of the partisan crowd. It didn't last long. Braking harshly for the Mulsanne corner on lap two, the all-French WM, with too much rear brake bias, slewed into a half spin. That wasn't the end of the matter, though. Dorchy proceeded to repass Wollek to lead the third lap – before wiping off his nose at Mulsanne corner. End of the glory for the under-financed little team, these days run out of Dorchy's garage. Both WMs were destined to retire, as was the other fast Mulsanne runner in C1, a March propelled by a turbocharged 3.4 litre Buick engine. High horsepower gave it high speed but it was too heavy and slow over the lap to concern the established turbocars.

With Dorchy gone, it still wasn't plain sailing for Wollek. He had a horde of Porsches in pursuit, with his sister car tagging along for good measure. It was a tremendously close race – and after two hours there were still 14 cars on the lead lap. Lancia wasn't hogging all the spotlight, but it was always right up in contention, a pattern that continued for 12 hours. Alas, only moments after half distance the Barilla/Baldi/Heyer car broke fifth gear. It took over three-quarters of an hour to repair. Four hours later Wollek/Nannini suffered the same fate.

Lancia's challenge had been stronger and longer-lived than most observers had predicted, but it was over, all the same. The only consolation came shortly afterwards when Team Manager Cesare Fiorio let Nannini have a crack at the lap record – which he duly snatched from the absent Ickx. The Wollek/Nannini car finally finished eighth after a second bout of transmission trouble killed hopes of a top six placing. The sister car of Baldi/Barilla/Heyer eventually expired with a broken distributor drive, having completed 275 laps. A third, back-up car entered by a French property company for Gabianni/Martini/Lapeyre broke its 2.65 litre engine overnight.

The widely predicted demise of the Lancia threat left the race as a Porsche parade, but in the absence of the factory team it was a more open contest than for many a year. And the boycott worked: shortly after the event FISA relented and resolved to implement a 15% reduced fuel ration rather than an IMSA-style formula for 1985.

Gunning for Stuttgart's win number nine (to equal Ferrari's all-time record) were no less than 16 privately-run cars, including entries from the top teams of the Kremer brothers, Reinhold Joest, John Fitzpatrick and Richard Lloyd. All the main runners were equipped with 650 b.h.p. Motronic engines, except for the three cars fielded by Joest, who relied upon mechanical injection and suffered an early setback when a fuel metering problem cost his number one car (Pescarolo/Ludwig) a lap. Later the number one Kremer car (Jones/Schuppan/Jarier) suffered a similar delay while leading, in this case the car's nose getting knocked off by the somewhat erratic Dorchy's WM.

Overnight Joest suffered a second, greater setback when Johansson crashed his second car on oil, but his lead entry was steadily regaining its lost ground. The solitary Canon car (Palmer/Lammers) had faded with a multitude of problems. Then the fastest Fitzpatrick car (Hobbs/van der Merwe/Streiff) suffered a power loss, probably due to a cracked cylinder. However, at three-quarter distance, in spite of the night's toll (which, of course, included the demise of the Lancias), it was still a tight race, albeit a three-horse one. The Pescarolo/Ludwig 956 had inherited the lead with the demise of the Wollek/Nannini Lancia, but it was less than four minutes ahead of the dark horse – a new 956 owned by Preston Henn and crewed by Paul Jnr/Rondeau/Henn. And the Jones/Schuppan/Jarier Kremer car was only one lap down.

Joest lost four minutes through a minor suspension problem, then regained the advantage when the Henn car required new pads. It was close stuff, but in the end the experienced team with its two former winners pulled through. The Kremer team lost its chance 90 minutes from the finish, when a piston crown melted. The car limped home to collect sixth place.

Remarkably, the top seven positions were filled by Porsche 956s – and eight examples finished, the lowest in ninth. Three examples were lost in accidents and one was disqualified for outside assistance. Of the four retirements, two were down to engine failures, two to electrical faults.

Hoping to have penetrated the Porsche ranks at the finish had been four gallant, normally-aspirated, British challengers – two Aston Martins and two Jaguars. This year the Cosworth-Ford runners were confined to the C2 class for any hope of success, although seven examples did run, unsuccessfully, in C1, representing Rondeau, Dome, Cougar, Lola and Grid. The Aston Martin representatives were familiar Nimrods, run by Viscount Downe's team and developed and prepared by Ray Mallock. The Nimrod factory having collapsed, Downe now had two chassis at his disposal. Although Mallock's own entry (shared with Olson) had lightened body panels, both cars were still well over 950kgs (let alone 850kgs) and the 5.3 V8 could still not muster 600 b.h.p. An experimental turbocharged derivative had proved to be more trouble than it was worth.

The Jaguars were American-built and prepared cars run by the Group 44 IMSA team with factory support in the form of technical assistance and finance. The project was the brainchild of Group 44 boss Bob Tullius, who had long experience of racing Coventry's 5.3 litre, two valves per cylinder, s.o.h.c. 60 degree V12 in the States. Tullius had commissioned top American designer Lee Dykstra to produce a ground effect, monocoque prototype chassis with Le Mans potential to house the long power plant back in 1982, so the 'XJR-5' had two years' race development behind it. By 1984 Group 44 had developed a long stroke 6.0 litre version of the Jaguar stock block, rated at over 600 b.h.p. and, with Lucas Micos engine management trickery, reckoned to be one of the must fuel efficient engines in the fuel-ration-free IMSA series. However, that engine put the XJR-5 in IMSA's 900kg class and even then the car couldn't be brought down to weight. The Jaguars were almost as heavy as the Downe Nimrods. Nevertheless, the marque was back in the Le Mans game, thanks to Tullius, and its commercial revival following its release from the shackles of Leyland Cars. The now-flourishing concern had no illusions about winning with its overweight, under-powered cars – it sought the development benefits that could lead to future success.

Tullius put a premium on experience and shared his car with Redman and Bundy, while entrusting the other to Watson, Ballot-Lena and Adamowicz – all except Bundy (35) and Watson (37) were over 40 years old. And prudence was the key note of qualifying, the team unconcerned when Mallock fitted qualifying tyres and clinched the normally aspirated pole.

Come the race, and Tullius had the satisfaction of leading a lap towards the end of the first hour as the turbocars ahead of him replenished. As the race settled down the Jaguars became well established in the top 10, running in close company with Mallock's Nimrod. Tragically, at 9.30 p.m. Mallock's sister car hit the barrier on the Mulsanne and his own collided with the wreckage. Both were wiped out and a track marshal lost his life in the incident, which brought out the pace car for just over an hour. Thereafter, the Jaguars hovered around sixth and seventh places until midnight, when Adamowicz brought no. 40 in with a chunked tyre, losing a place. At half distance, however, the Coventry cats were again sixth and seventh. Alas, soon after 4.00 a.m. there was yet more trouble for 40: first a broken throttle cable, then a deflating tyre which pitched it into the barrier. The car limped back to the pits but its oil tank had been ruptured and the engine had seized.

Car 44 continued to hold down sixth place until soon after 7.00 a.m., when third gear stripped. It was a repeat of a failure which had occurred during a 24-hour trial at Pocono in the USA and which had been wrongly diagnosed. The delay dropped the car to 10th place, but by 10.00 a.m. a top six position was once more on the cards. Alas, with just over three hours to run, the gearbox seized, probably due to debris from the broken gear blocking an oil-way. It was the end of the road, but not the end of Jaguar's Le Mans ambitions in the Eighties.

1.	2.6t Porsche* (Pescarolo/Ludwig)	6.	2.6t Porsche (Jones/Schuppan/Jarier)	
2.	2.6t Porsche (Rondeau/Paul/Henn)		* Class winner. Also:	
3.	2.6t Porsche (Hobbs/Streiff/van der Merwe)	10.	1.3 Lola-Mazda (Morton/Katayama/O'Steen)	
4.	2.6t Porsche (Brun/Akin/von Bayern)	14.	3.5 BMW (Kon/Dagoreau/Thoisy)	
5.	2.6t Porsche (Merl/Winter/Schornstein)	17.	3.0 Porsche (Perrier/Touroul/Bertapella)	

1985

Both Lancia and Jaguar came to La Sarthe with renewed hope. Lancia had a more effective engine management system for its 3.0 litre engine (still bigger than the flat sixes fielded by Porsche), improved aerodynamics and suspension (adapted to Michelin radials) and, most significant of all, a new, stronger gearbox. Jaguar also had an improved challenger, with more power (650 b.h.p. on the dyno – as high as the levels used by the Group C turbocars), if still suffering a 100kgs weight penalty. The overdue imposition of the 2,210 litre fuel ration promised to help the Coventry cause. Group 44 team chief Tullius made it clear that his objective was to win, but things turned sour from the very first day of qualifying. Wednesday evening cost the V12 power plant in both cars. The compulsory fuel supply took the blame and the timing was backed off to avoid the risk of further detonation – at the expense of fuel economy.

Lancia was expected to dominate practice, as it had done at previous races, using costly qualifying engines. But on this occasion the works Porsche team joined in the game and confined the Italian challenge to the second row. Nevertheless, Wollek drove his Lancia LC2-85 between the long wheelbase 962C *langhecks* of Ickx and Bell at the first corner to seize the initiative: but only because the factory Porsche team had A Plan. And Wollek only led for three laps before surrendering his prime TV shot, falling back behind four private Porsches as he, too, adjusted to a predetermined pace.

Lancia's chosen gait wasn't uncompetitive, though. For the first 12 hours Wollek/Nannini/Cesario held a top six position amid the Porsches, a few places ahead of the sister car of Pescarolo/Baldi. Alas, not long after 3.00 a.m., a damaged turbo wastegate cost half-an-hour and a top 10 placing. Three hours later the sister car hit a variety of small problems so that by Sunday morning, with both cars over 10 laps behind the leading Porsche, the marque's chances were shot. Setbacks to some of the top 10 Porsches eventually allowed the Ferrari-engined rivals into sixth and seventh places: at least this year the cars from Turin saw the finish.

Jaguar had the same satisfaction even if it, likewise, hadn't lived up to its 1984 promise. It wasn't long before both cars were eased back in the interests of fuel economy and just after half distance the second car rolled to a halt with a broken c.v. joint. The battery ran down providing lights to warn of the hazard as Adam isolated the half shaft and did not have enough juice left to re-start the engine.

Jaguar tested the water at Le Mans in 1984, then came back aiming to win in 1985. For a variety of reasons it did not extract sufficient speed from its American-run entries. Photo: John Overton.

Tullius/Robinson/Ballot-Lena lost 40 minutes with two changes of engine electrics on Sunday morning, but with 90 minutes to run a top 10 placing still looked on the cards. That was the moment when hopes dived: the car came in with water dripping from the exhaust pipe. A valve had hit a piston. The offending cylinder was carefully sealed off and Tullius waited patiently to limp around to the chequered flag. The 11 cylinder car went so well he arrived too early and had to do a second lap, but car 44 made it, classified 13th.

Jaguar's welcome finish was two places behind Aston Martin's best. The smaller British manufacturer no longer had a budget for racing but Tickford continued to supply the EMKA and Cheetah single car outfits with its 570 b.h.p. V8. Sadly, the Swiss Cheetah effort was fraught with problems, but the EMKA, absent due to lack of sponsorship in '84, outqualified the Jaguars. Enthusiastically driven by Needell, the now flat bottom warrior with impressive Mulsanne speed became the surprise of the first hour – within the first 30 minutes it had charged into a remarkable third place. After 48 minutes of this spirited activity it dived into the pits – where it waited only long enough for half a tank of fuel. The upshot of this was that after the turbocars had all pitted (and some of the pussy-footing Porsches went a lap beyond the hour), EMKA came into its own.

After three (carefully contrived) laps of glory, Aston Martin's representative settled down on the verge of the top 10, behind the troublefree turbocars but ahead of the Jaguars, and ahead of the Coventry challenge it stayed all the way to the finish, overcoming a problem on Sunday morning with the clutch, and a fractured fuel line in the afternoon.

So by 3.00 p.m. on Sunday there was some sense of achievement enjoyed by Lancia, Jaguar and, most of all, by EMKA/Aston Martin. But the glory in the C1 class was again monopolized by Porsche. WM was represented by three cars this year, Rondeau by four but the home runners lacked speed and stamina – as did two newcomers from the orient: Dome chassis propelled by underpowered 2.1 litre Toyota turbo engines. Porsche had such a grip on C1 that a March and the works Cougar both, unsuccessfully, used Porsche turbo engines. Surprisingly, the three works cars were overshadowed in the race by the pick of the marque's privateers. In the early stages this was out of choice: the works drivers had those instructions to pussy-foot. As early as 3.30 p.m. two of the private 956s had drawn out a clear advantage. These were the '84 winning Joest car (with its Joest-prepared engine, suspected to be of 3.0 litre capacity, cockpit adjustable fuel mixture and ultra-low drag aerodynamics) crewed by Ludwig/Barilla and the unique aluminium honeycomb sandwich monocoque 956/106B fielded by Richard Lloyd's Canon team and entrusted to Palmer/Weaver.

Ludwig and Palmer had quickly established a rapport, taking turns to slipstream each other down the Mulsanne, thereby saving fuel. Setting the pace, neither was forcing it. Coming upon the pit stop-delayed Tullius, they were content to shadow him, catching on speed only to lose out again to the V12's torque. Moving swiftly, the Porsche drivers were not being lead footed. As the race settled into a pattern, cars 7 (Joest) and 14 (Canon) remained elusively ahead of the rest of the turbo train – and showed themselves to be two of the most fuel efficient, to boot. At around quarter-distance the pace car came out for half-an-hour following a barrier-damaging shunt on the Mulsanne and Louis Krages (alias John Winter) took his first stint in the Joest car. Accepting that he didn't have the pace of Ludwig and Barilla he agreed to act as reserve driver for the duration.

While Winter had been following one of the pace cars, the rival Canon machine had started to misfire. A switch of Motronics black box didn't do the trick – the problem was subsequently traced to false information sent by a faulty water temperature sensor, which was duly disconnected. The delay found the car in seventh position at midnight and the remaining 15 hours were spent in a splendid recovery to the runner-up position, while the Joest car swept serenely on towards victory, shrugging off the best efforts of the factory team, to arrive home with 140 litres to spare.

In the early stages the Weissach-prepared cars had been driven so carefully that they fell right out of the top 10. Then Ickx/Mass suffered a transmission malady and electrical woes, losing five laps. However, around quarter-distance Bell/Stuck and Holbert/Schuppan/Watson speeded up, to claim second and third places in the wake of the Canon team's problems. By this stage the third works car had been further delayed by a total gearbox rebuild.

Sunday quickly threw wheel bearing failure at the second and third placed Porsches but the Holbert/Schuppan/Watson car which suffered the shortest delay quickly made amends, to regain second by half distance. Another wheelbearing failure at 8.30 a.m. cost it that place, and later in the morning it broke its crankshaft. The Bell/Stuck entry, which had needed a complete change of upright, at least salvaged third place, some six laps down, while the badly delayed Ickx/Mass car steadily regained ground to take 10th place.

At no stage had the factory cars looked like seriously unsettling Joest's 956-117's bid to become only the second-ever car to win Le Mans in successive years. The works team had been well humbled – but it was a great day for the marque, which now held the all-time record of Le Mans wins: 10.

1.	2.6t Porsche* (Ludwig/Barilla/Winter)	6.	3.0t Lancia (Wollek/Nannini/Cesario)
2.	2.6t Porsche (Palmer/Weaver/Lloyd)		* Class winner. Also:
3.	2.6t Porsche (Bell/Stuck)	13.	6.0 Jaguar (Tullius/Robinson/Ballot-Lena)
4.	2.6t Porsche (Hobbs/Edwards/Gartner)	14.	3.3 Tiga-Ford (Spice/Bellm/Galvin)
5.	2.6t Porsche (Hytten/van der Merwe/Fouche)	15.	3.5 BMW (Doren/Birrane/Libert)

1986

A Jaguar victory once more, after all those years? British enthusiasts swarmed over as never before, inspired by a fine victory for the Coventry-commissioned, ART-built, TWR-run XJR-6 V12 racer at Silverstone earlier in the month. Success so early in the marque's World Championship programme hadn't been anticipated. Mind you, Le Mans was a different nut to crack, particularly as the ACO had significantly increased the Group C fuel allocation from 2,210 litres to 2,550 litres, a 15% jump. The hot new four-valve turbo engine pace was a fraction higher than that comfortable for the two-valve Big Cats. However, not all of the 14-strong Porsche army was on it. In fact, only three familiar Stuttgart cars went out ahead of the three British-built, sophisticated carbonfibre monocoque runners (which left Porsche lagging in terms of chassis engineering) – Joest's famous two times winning 956 and the lead factory 962s. And Le Mans is not only about speed. So often do the swift stumble. For sure TWR was keeping a little in reserve on its first visit to La Sarthe. But strength comes with experience. There again, luck knows no logic...

Cheever's third row time had nothing to do with luck. It was the most impressive normally aspirated performance of the Group C turbo era and a great tribute to the engine development work done by Jaguar in association with Group 44 and TWR, and to ART's Tony Southgate's excellent, light Dunlop-shod chassis. Weight, tyres and lack of Group C experience had always been Group 44's handicaps. Running close to the minimum weight limit on the same tyres as the works Porsche team and learning fast, the new Jaguar bid was something else...

But Jaguar didn't plan to win. Coventry was hoping, *realistically* to win on its third attempt with TWR. First time around, second time around would be a bonus. So the promising fourth place held by Cheever/Warwick/Schlesser on Saturday was particularly pleasing. More so because the sister cars (Heyer/Redman/Haywood and Brancatelli/Percy/Hahne) were close behind. For three-and-a-half hours. Then Heyer stopped at Indianapolis, fuel in the tank but fuel pressure gone. Four hours: Porsche – Porsche – Porsche – one lap – Jaguar – Jaguar. Not a great deal to lose over four hours, one lap. Six hours: two laps. Still not a great deal. Jaguar might lack winning pace but the three leaders couldn't afford to stumble at all...

The fourth-place Jaguar stumbled first, an electrical problem costing 15 minutes. But still the sister car continued the good work, until 2.00 a.m. That was when an outer c.v. joint failed, giving Percy a big moment.

The surviving car's joints were given extra lubrication at each stop, just in case. Then it was the turn of the Porsches to stumble. Two of them. At breakfast time on Sunday the Jaguar was second, albeit eight laps in arrears to the leading factory car. With another third of the race to run anything could happen. And something soon did. At 8.35 a.m. a Dunlop tyre blew the chances of a marque. It could so easily have been that of the works Porsche. But such is the way of fate.

This weekend fate was not just unkind, it was cruel, claiming the life of Kremer Porsche driver Gartner just before half distance. The pace cars came out for over two hours and Le Mans became a joyless drive home for the factory car of Bell/Stuck/Holbert. Prior to the tragedy the race had been a humdinger, the eventual winner slugging it out with the Joest's remarkable Old Number 7 (again crewed by Ludwig/Barilla/Winter) in a way that brought to mind Ickx and Herrmann in '69. Except that this time the excitement lasted for almost half the race. And the protagonists were never far ahead of the other fast factory 962 in the hands of Wollek/Mass/Schuppan. This was no staged affair. The year before Joest had shown that the factory team was *not* unbeatable. This year Weissach had already lost its third 962 with trick clutchless transmission (Schuppan/Olson). Early on, the transmission broke. It lost the third place car just before the Gartner accident, Mass crashing on oil. But the Porsche factory always runs three cars as one, statistically, will go the distance. Sure enough, the dice now fell against Joest. Running behind the pace car its engine seized.

The Joest team had a second 956, for steady Americans Follmer/Morton/Miller. Retirements among the faster Porsches and Jaguars left them third at the finish. There was only one private Porsche that had been close to race pace left at the end, the Brun car of Larrauri/Gouhier/Pareja, in second spot and eight laps behind the leader (having suffered a broken suspension rocker arm). The same team's Boutsen/Ferte/Theys car had shown strongly in the early stages, only for Ferte to crash. And its third car in the hands of Brun/Sigala/Jelinski had early on dropped a valve. The other favoured private Porsche team was that of Kremer, which withdrew its second car, having lost Gartner...

The TWR Jaguars took over the Coventry challenge from Group 44 in 1986. Better prepared for Le Mans thanks to greater experience of getting the best out of the V12 within the constraints of Group C regulations, the team gave a splendid account of itself. Ultimate retirement for both cars was no disgrace upon a first visit to La Sarthe. Photo: John Overton.

The top five was rounded out by the Fitzpatrick team (of which the second car took tenth) and the Obermeier team, while the other Porsche 956/962 present, the honeycomb chassis car that had finished second the previous year, could manage no better than ninth, leased to the Liqui Moly team.

While the professional Porsche Group C teams managed to field only five relatively trouble-free runners from all those entries, German dentist and historic racer Siggi Brunn ran the ex-Joest '82 936C without hassle to collect sixth place. If Brunn's chassis was an old-stager, its (under-powered) engine was brand new: a factory-loaned two-valve 3.0 litre destined for use the following season under more restrictive IMSA regulations. Next up was another interesting Porsche development, a 4-w-d '961' 200-off homologation GT special, the most radical 911 derivative ever to emerge from Stuttgart. Its run was relatively smooth and had the weather been in its favour (say, with a blizzard) it might have made it into the top six.

Of three Porsche-powered Group C specials in the race (two Marches and a Cougar), one March finished to win GTP with 14th position – close behind an outclassed Rondeau-Cosworth. Almost all the Rondeau and WMs had made the smart move into Group C2.

Although Porsche was still fully in command of Group C1, fellow Stuttgart marque Mercedes and three Japanese factories, Nissan, Mazda and Toyota, were cautiously queuing behind Jaguar hoping to take a swipe at it.

Mercedes' effort was a low-key one, officially a private venture by tuner Heini Mader and constructor Peter Sauber. They fielded two lightly turbocharged 5.0 litre V8-propelled Sauber C-8s but both suffered engine failure early in the race, never having looked a strong threat.

The six-car Japanese force was no more competitive, in spite of high power claims for the Nissan 3.0 V6 turbos powering two Nissan-sponsored Marches. Neither Nissan was on the pace and only one finished, sneaking into 17th place, 11 laps behind an underpowered 2.1 turbo Dome-Toyota survivor. Toyota lost one car, Mazda lost both, so none of the oriental teams had anything to be proud of. Nevertheless, the intent was there and all planned to be back with more competitive machinery. Given the Japanese motor industry's excellent track record in international motor racing, the seeds of Porsche's downfall might have drifted in from the East . . .

1.	2.6t Porsche* (Bell/Stuck/Holbert)	6.	3.0t Joest-Porsche (Brunn/Seher/Schuster)
2.	2.6t Porsche (Larrauri/Paraja/Gouhier)		* Class winner. Also:
3.	2.6t Porsche (Follmer/Morton/Miller)	7.	2.8t Porsche (Metge/Ballot-Lena)
4.	2.6t Porsche (de Villota/Velez/Fouche)	8.	3.3 Gebhardt-Ford (Harrower/Clements/Dodd-Noble)
5.	2.6t Porsche (Laessig/Ballabio/Wood)	14.	2.8t March-Porsche (Robert/Newsum/Cleare)
		20.	3.5 BMW (Libert/Witmeur/Krankenburg)

YEAR	MARQUE	CYL. (c.c.)	DISTANCE (kms)	DRIVERS	AV'AGE SPEED (k.p.h.)	FASTEST LAP (k.p.h.)	INDEX OF PERFORMANCE	NO. PARTICI-P'NTS	RE-TIRE-M'TS
1923	Chenard & Walcker	2978	2209,536	Lagache Léonard	92,064	*Bentley* 107,328		33	3
1924	Bentley	2995	2077,340	Duff Clement	86,555	Lagache *Chenard & Walcker* 111,168		40	23
1925	La Lorraine	3473	2233,982	de Courcelles Rossignol	93,082	Lagache *Chenard & Walcker* 112,987		49	33
1926	La Lorraine	3440	2552,414	Bloch Rossignol	106,350	de Courcelles *La Lorraine* 114,444	O.M. (Minoia-Foresti)	41	28
1927	Bentley	2989	2369,807	Benjafield Davis	98,740	*Bentley* 118,148 118,148	SALMSON (Casse-Rousseau)	22	15
1928	Bentley	4392	2669,272	Barnato Rubin	111,219	Birkin *Bentley* 127,604	SALMSON (Caese-Rousseau)	33	16
1929	Bentley	6597	2843,830	Barnato Birkin	118,492	Birkin *Bentley* 133,551	BENTLEY (Barnato-Birkin)	25	15
1930	Bentley	6597	2930,663	Barnato Kidston	122,111	Birkin *Bentley* 144,352	TALBOT (Lewis-Eaton)	18	9
1931	Alfa-Romeo	2337	3017,654	Lord Howe Birkin	125,735	Ivanowski *Mercédès* 129,234	ALFA-ROMEO (Howe-Birkin)	26	17
1932	Alfa-Romeo	2377	2954,038	Sommer Chinetti	123,084	Minoia *Alfa-Roméo* 142,437	ALFA-ROMEO (Sommer Chinetti)	25	16
1933	Alfa-Romeo	2336	3144,038	Nuvolari Sommer	131,001	Sommer *Alfa-Roméo* 146,386	RILEY (Von der Becke Peacock)	29	14
1934	Alfa-Romeo	2336	2886,938	Chinetti Etancelin	120,289	Etancelin *Alfa-Roméo* 142,437	RILEY (Von der Becke Peacock)	44	21
1935	Lagonda	2451	3006,797	Hindmarsh Fontes	125,283	Howe *Alfa-Roméo* 139,612	ASTON MARTIN (Martin Brackenbury)	58	30
1937	Bugatti	3266	3287,938	Wimille Benoist	136,997	Wimille *Bugatti* 155,179	BUGATTI (Wimille-Benoist)	48	31
1938	Delahaye	3558	3180,940	Chaboud Tremoulet	132,539	Sommer *Alfa-Roméo* 154,783	SIMCA (Aimé-Plantivaux)	42	27
1939	Bugatti	3251	3354,760	Wimille Veyron	139,781	Mazaud *Delahaye* 155,627	SIMCA (Gordini-Scaron)	42	22
1949	Ferrari	1995	3178,299	Lord Selsdon Chinetti	132,420	Simon *Delahaye* 155,427	FERRARI (Lord Selsdon-Chinetti)	49	30
1950	Talbot	4483	3465,120	Rosier Louis Rosier J.-L.	144,380	Louis Rosier *Talbot* 165,480	*ex aequo:* MONOPOLE (de Montrèmy-Hemard) ASTON MARTIN (Abbecassis-Macklin)	60	32
1951	Jaguar	3441	3611,193	Walker Whitehead	150,466	Moss *Jaguar* 169,356	MONOPOLE (de Montrèmy-Hemard)	60	30
1952	Mercédès-Benz	2996	3733,800	Lang Riess	155,575	Ascari *Ferrari* 173,159	PANHARD (Hemard-Dessous)	57	40
1953	Jaguar	3441	4088,064	Rolt Hamilton	170,336	Ascari *Ferrari* 181,642	PANHARD (Chancel-Chancel)	60	34
1954	Ferrari	4954	4061,150	Gonzalès Trintignant	169,215	Marzotto *Ferrari* 189,139	D.B. (Bonnet-Bayol)	57	40
1955	Jaguar	3442	4135,380	Hawthorn Bueb	172,308	Hawthorn *Jaguar* 196,963	PORSCHE (Polensky-Von Frankenberg)	60	39
1956	Jaguar	3442	4034,929	Flockhart Sanderson	168,122	Hawthorn *Jaguar* 186,383	D.B. (Laureau-Armagnac)	52	38
1957	Jaguar	3781	4397,108	Flockhart Bueb	183,217	Hawthorn *Ferrari* 203,015	LOTUS (Allison-Hall)	54	34
1958	Ferrari	2953	4101,926	P. Hill Gendebien	170,914	Hawthorn *Ferrari* 195,402	OSCA (de Tomaso-Colin Davis)	55	35

Year	Make			Drivers					
1959	Aston-Martin	2993	4347,900	Salvadori Shelby	181,163	Behra *Ferrari* 201,161	D.B. (Cornet-Cotton)	53	40
1960	Ferrari	2958	4217,527	Frère Gendebien	175,730	Gregory *Maserati* 198,605	D.B. (Laureau-Armagnac)	55	35
1961	Ferrari	2961	4476,580	Gendebien P. Hill	186,527	R. Rodriguez *Ferrari* 201,202	D.B. (Laureau-Bouharde)	55	33
1962	Ferrari	3926	4451,225	Gendebien P. Hill	185,469	P. Hill *Ferrari* 204,202	PANHARD C.D. (Guilhaudin-Bertaut)	55	37
1963	Ferrari	2953	4561,170	Scarfiotti Bandini	190,071	Surtees *Ferrari* 207,714	FERRARI (Scarfiotti-Bandini)	49	36
1964	Ferrari	3299	4695,310	Guichet Vaccarella	195,638	P. Hill *Ford* 211,429	FERRARI (Guichet-Vaccarella)	55	30
1965	Ferrari	3286	4677,110	Gregory Rindt	194,880	P. Hill *Ford* 222,803	PORSCHE (Linge-Nöcker)	51	37
1966	Ford	6982	4843,090	Amon McLaren	201,196	Gurney *Ford* 230,103	PORSCHE (Davis-Siffert)	55	40
1967	Ford	6980	5232,900	Gurney A. J. Foyt	218,038	Hulme *Ford* 238,014	PORSCHE (Siffert-Herrmann)	54	38
1968	Ford	4942	4452,880	P. Rodriguez Bianchi	185,536	Siffert *Porsche* 210,631	ALPINE RENAULT (Nicolas-Andruet)	54	36
1969	Ford	4942	4998,000	Ickx Oliver	208,250	Elford *Porsche* 234,017	ALPINE RENAULT (Serpaggi-Ethuin)	45	31
1970	Porsche	4494	4607,810	Attwood Herrmann	191,992	Elford *Porsche* 241,235	PORSCHE (Lins-Marco)	51	35
1971	Porsche	4907	5335,313	Marko Van Lennep	222,304	Siffert *Porsche* 243,905	PORSCHE (Marko-Van Lennep)	59	35
1972	Matra	2993	4691,343	Pescarolo G. Hill	195,472	Van Lennep *Lola T 290* 216,413		55	36
1973	Matra	2993	4853,945	Pescarolo Larrousse	202,247	Cevert *Matra* 223,607		55	34
1974	Matra	2993	4606,571	Pescarolo Larrousse	191,940	Jarier *Matra* 220,494		49	29
1975	Gulf Ford	2986	4595,577	Ickx Bell	191,482	Craft *De Cadenet* 210,026		55	25
1976	Porsche	2998	4769,923	Ickx Van Lennep	198,746	Jabouille *Renault-Alpine* 220,197		55	28
1977	Porsche	2998	4671,630	Barth Haywood Ickx	194,651	Ickx *Porsche* 226,494		55	34
1978	Renault	2796	5044,530	Pironi Jaussaud	210,188	Jabouille *Renault* 229,244		55	31
1979	Porsche	4190	4173,930	Ludwig Whittington, D. Whittington, B.	173,913	Ickx *Porsche* 227,003		55	33
1980	Rondeau	2993	4608,020	Rondeau Jaussaud	192,000	Ickx *Porsche* 222,373		55	30
1981	Porsche	3708	4825,348	Ickx Bell	201,056	Haywood *Porsche* 229,231		55	35
1982	Porsche	3708	4899,086	Ickx Bell	204,128	Ragnotti *Rondeau* 226,157		55	36
1983	Porsche	3708	5041,620	Holbert Haywood Schuppan	210,070	Ickx *Porsche* 233,922		51	30
1984	Porsche	3708	4900,280	Pescarolo Ludwig	204.180	Wollek *Porsche* 234.820		53	31
1985	Porsche	3708	5088,507	Ludwig Barilla Winter	211,880	Mass *Porsche* 239,161		54	30
1986	Porsche	3708	4972,730	Stuck Bell Holbert	207.197	Ludwig *Porsche* 239,560		50	31